face to face

CHILDREN OF THE AIDS CRISIS IN AFRICA

PHOTOGRAPHY | KAREN ANDE
STORY | RUTHANN RICHTER

FOREWORD | PETER PIOT

Copyright © 2010 by Karen Ande and Ruthann Richter

All rights reserved. No part of this book may be reproduced by any means, in any media, electronic or mechanical, including motion picture film, video, photocopy, recording or any other information storage retrieval system, without permission in writing from the authors.

For information, address:
Hope Publishing House
P. O. Box 60008
Pasadena, CA 91116 – USA
Tel: (626)792-6123 / Fax: (626)792-2121
HopePublishingHouse@gmail.com
www.hope-pub.com

Printed in Canada on acid-free paper.

Book design by Clark Creative Group
San Francisco, CA

Library of Congress Cataloging-in-Publication Data
Ande, Karen, 1950–
    Face to face : children of the AIDS crisis in Africa / photography, Karen Ande ; story, Ruthann Richter ; foreword, Peter Piot.
      p. cm.
  ISBN 978-1-932717-20-4 (pbk. : alk. paper)
  1. Orphans–Kenya–Social conditions. 2. Orphans–Services for–Kenya. 3. Children of AIDS patients–Kenya–Social conditions. 4. AIDS (Disease)–Social aspects–Kenya. I. Richter, Ruthann, 1952– II. Title.
    HV1346.5.A53 2010
    362.73096762--dc22   2009029870

THE EAGER STUDENTS AT MAMA DARLENE
CHILDREN'S CENTRE, TALA, KENYA

contents

Foreword 1

Introduction 4

Tales from Tala 10

Gilgil: The Survivors 24

Esther's World 38

Priestly Blessings 48

Kibera: Nairobi's Underbelly 60

Growing Up with HIV 76

Go Go Grannies: Africa's Well of Hope 88

Mama Natasha and Her Brood 102

A Brief Chronology of the Epidemic 116

Acknowledgements 118

About the Author and Photographer 120

Resources 121

foreword

It is remarkable how far we have come since the early 1980s, when I was a scientist studying the beginnings of the AIDS epidemic in central Africa. AIDS has since been recognized as the defining social, economic and political issue of our time. We have made great strides in terms of the science, prevention and treatment of AIDS and have marshaled substantial resources to deal with this unprecedented human crisis.

Where we have fallen short, however, is in our support for the millions of children affected by the pandemic. In our accelerated global response to AIDS, children largely have been left behind, particularly in the hard-hit region of sub-Saharan Africa, home to some 22 million people with HIV. As adults die, the children are adrift; they no longer can count on traditional family and social networks, which have collapsed under the weight of the epidemic. These youngsters come to lack life's essentials—food and shelter—and suffer psychosocial problems that hamper their development. Some have to grapple with HIV infection themselves.

There are now an estimated 12 million children in sub-Saharan Africa who have lost one or both parents to AIDS, and this figure grows by the day. These children receive little in the way of outside support: fewer than 10 percent of the extended families that support orphans and vulnerable children are reached by either community or government-funded programs. And while we have succeeded in scaling up treatment, with 4 million people now on antiretroviral drugs, children with HIV are far less likely to obtain this life-giving therapy. At best, one of every 10 youngsters with the disease has access to these valuable, AIDS-fighting medications.

This book brings these issues to the forefront, providing seldom-seen and poignant portraits of the lives of children in sub-Saharan Africa who are growing up in the world of AIDS. These are remarkably resilient youngsters, children with the faces of hope, carrying on in the face of daunting loss and economic deprivation. While they all too often must survive on their own, some remarkable people have mobilized at the grassroots level to support these youngsters, and this book also introduces us to them. They are living testimony to how change can happen when individuals and communities respond. I learned the value of activism early on in my career. I know one person or action can change the lives of many. The activists in this book have enhanced the lives of thousands.

We are now at a crossroads in the epidemic. It has become clear that AIDS is a long-term phenomenon that will challenge the very existence of families and even entire communities in Africa for decades to come. With that realization must come a new framework for action.

We must recast our global response to the epidemic to place greater emphasis on children. That means investing in rebuilding families and overtaxed communities to insure that orphans and vulnerable children receive adequate support. It means mobilizing the ability of AIDS organizations, health and social systems, and community networks to embrace responses tailored to children's needs. It means moving children from the back-burner to the center of the public policy agenda to help preserve the well-being of the next generation. We owe that to the children—and to ourselves. They are not only our responsibility. They are also our future.

– Prof. Peter Piot
Director of the Institute for Global Health at Imperial College, London, and former executive director of the Joint United Nations Programme on HIV/AIDS (UNAIDS)

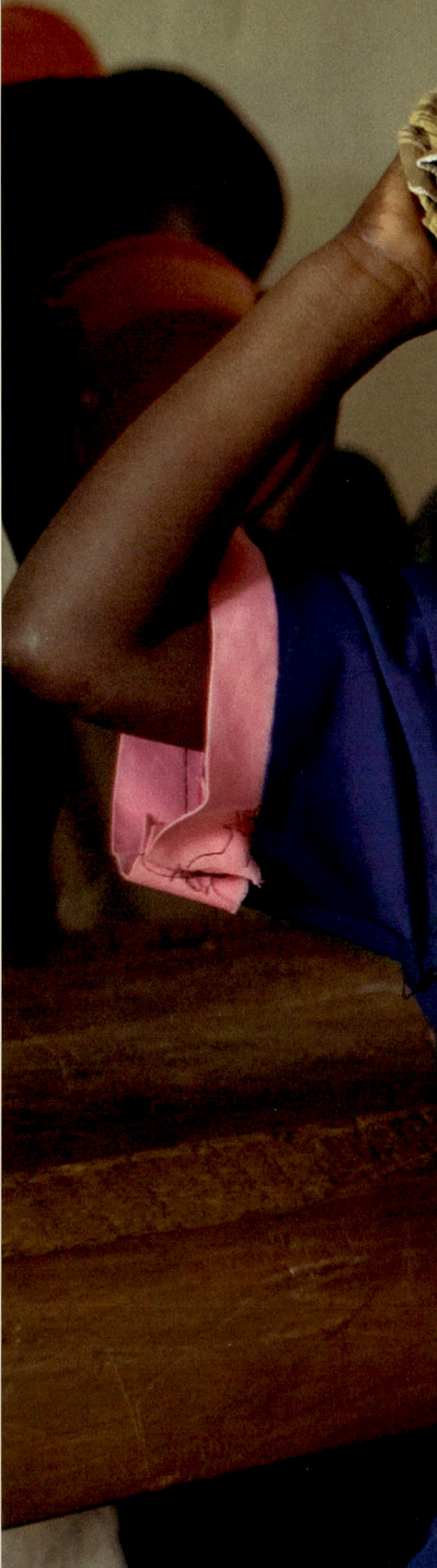

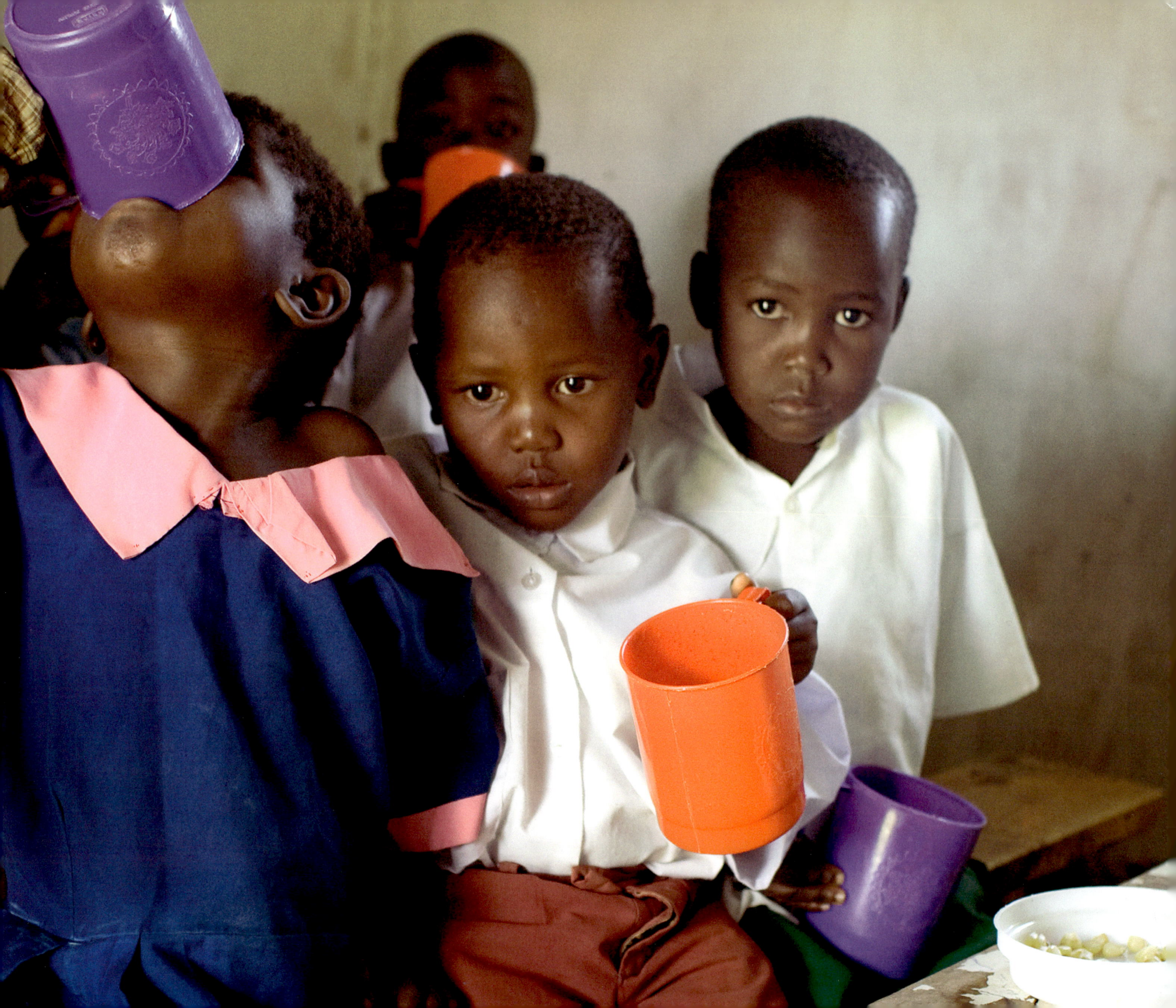

introduction

We arrived in a cloud of dust in rural Tala, as 60 children in red-checked uniforms lifted their arms and voices in a joyful Swahili welcome song. I knew that behind each of these shining faces at Mama Darlene Children's Centre, there was a tragic tale to tell—of time spent grieving for family members whose lives had been drained by AIDS. And so I stood there and cried, a bit of an awkward moment for a visitor being so warmly embraced by this resilient little community in the East African bush.

That was how I began my odyssey across Kenya in 2004 with documentary photographer Karen Ande: We had come to gather the stories of these youngsters and their families so that the world might stand up on their behalf. For sadly, these children—and the 12 million others like them in sub-Saharan Africa—are among the neediest, most neglected, children on the planet. While their families and communities are crumbling around them, they must carry on under extraordinarily challenging circumstances, often deprived of food, a secure home, an education, basic health care and most importantly, the love and nurturing of a parent.

These children are the innocent bystanders in the global war on AIDS, which is destroying the social fabric in sub-Saharan Africa. For decades, the virus festered in the region while the world stood by, paralyzed by indifference. Meanwhile, the numbers grew to epic proportions, becoming a human catastrophe unprecedented in history. Today, two-thirds of the world's people living with HIV—an estimated 22 million adults and children—live in sub-Saharan Africa, only a fraction of them benefiting from the expensive, life-giving drugs that have made AIDS a manageable disease in the West. In 2007 alone, 1.5 million people in the region died of AIDS-related complications, according to the Joint United Nations Programme on HIV/AIDS (UNAIDS). Meanwhile, the number of children without parents will swell to more than 20 million by the year 2010, about the population of the entire continent of Australia.

MAMA DARLENE CHILDREN'S CENTRE

Although government and private organizations today are committing billions to combat the disease and prevent its spread, the response has come much too late, and precious few resources ever reach orphans and other youngsters living on the edge.

"Children and families have been shamefully neglected," said Linda Richter [no relation to author], a developmental psychologist at the Human Sciences Research Council in South Africa. She spoke to thousands of participants at the 2008 International AIDS Conference in Mexico City in what was, astonishingly, the first plenary session of the 23-year-old conference that was dedicated to children's issues.

Photographer Karen Ande first seized on the issue in 2002. She was traveling to Kenya to visit the game parks and do an assignment for a San Francisco Bay Area nonprofit working with youngsters in Kibera, Nairobi's notorious slum. She landed in the Kenyan capital after a 20-hour flight and while her companions headed to comfortable beds at the hotel, she trucked off to the gritty alleyways of Kibera. A rag-tag group of kids, many of them orphans, tumbled out of a corrugated metal shack,

JOYCE NDUKU (LEFT) AND FRIENDS SING A WELCOME SONG.

dressed in colorful hand-me-down clothes. They were laughing and shy around the sleepy white woman, who caught an image of a girl about five years old who had a regal look, tossing her magnificent braids back against the glinting sun.

The following week, Karen would visit a makeshift children's shelter in the Rift Valley town of Naivasha that was housed in what had been a school room at the local Catholic Church. There she photographed 3-year-old Samuel, who had been abandoned by his mother in a line at the hospital pharmacy. Samuel mugged for Karen's camera, but his brave smile could not entirely hide the sad truth. He was to go hungry that day because the shelter had run out of rice. He was one of dozens of children whom Karen photographed on that trip. After she returned to San Francisco, she watched his face and the faces of other vulnerable children emerge in her developing tray and resolved to find a way to put some food into their stomachs.

She hooked up with several other nonprofit organizations in the Bay Area and began mounting exhibits at community centers, public libraries, government buildings and churches. She spoke to schools, religious and community groups—anyone who would listen. And she was dogged in raising funds to support small, grassroots organizations in Africa that help these youngsters, collecting some $70,000 to date.

She hoped to broaden her reach by collaborating on these efforts with a writer. She turned to me, her longtime friend and former graduate school roommate at Stanford University. As a medical writer, I had covered AIDS for a daily newspaper in the Bay Area in the early days of the epidemic in the 1980s, when this strange disease had no name. In 1992, I joined the writing staff at the University of California, San Francisco, which was at the forefront of the world's effort to understand, treat and prevent HIV infection. The impact of AIDS became startlingly real, as I would regularly visit with patients at Ward 86, the clinic at the university-affiliated San Francisco General Hospital and ground zero for the U.S. epidemic.

But nothing in my experience would prepare me for what I would witness on that first trip to East Africa with Karen in 2004. We traveled to Kenya together on two other occasions, in 2005 and 2007, and Karen has gone on her own six times in the last eight years. One afternoon, we stopped by the government hospital in Naivasha, where officials reluctantly allowed us to peek inside a stark, dormitory-style AIDS ward that overflowed with dying patients, some two to three to a bed. The officials had nothing to offer these patients except palliative care. Antiretroviral drugs, then universally available in the West, were just trickling into Africa. The hospital had fewer than 500 doses to serve its population of 250,000 people in a region hard-hit by the disease, officials told us.

Less than a mile from the hospital, we saw other repercussions of this global policy of neglect. We headed down one of Naivasha's potholed, unpaved roads to visit 13-year-old Esther, who was nursing her dying mother in the family's one-room tin shack. The mother was a wasted slip of a woman with AIDS-associated tuberculosis; she would die three weeks after our visit. In addition to looking after her mother, Esther was responsible for three young brothers who were shoeless, dressed in tattered clothes and starved for food, affection and other essentials of life. She met the challenge with a dignity and grace that I would not have imagined possible in a teenager.

INTRODUCTION

From there, we headed north to a newly minted orphanage in the Rift Valley town of Gilgil. There we spent time with two-year-old Mary, who had been living with her 4-year-old sister under a lean-to of plastic and cardboard. Mary's parents had died of AIDS, leaving them in the hands of an absent, alcoholic grandfather. Before arriving at the orphanage, Mary was so profoundly traumatized that she did not speak and was literally crippled by malnutrition, barely able to move around on her knees. During our visit, she ran through the dirt courtyard of the orphanage, screeching with laughter.

Fortunately these and other children fell into good hands. For we encountered many bright spots in our travels—the activists who have rescued many youngsters from a precarious existence. They are children's advocates like Jill Simpson, the retired nurse who brought Mary to the orphanage. They are community organizers like Monica Ngumi, a powerful force of nature who offered sustenance to the motherless children who greeted me in Tala with their vibrant song of life. They are community leaders like Father Daniel Kiriti, a priest turned AIDS activist who has rescued abandoned children from the streets and who preaches HIV prevention in an effort to slow the tide of death. They are the grannies who have been pressed back into parenthood after the death of their children. And they are the children themselves who so often have to care for their brothers and sisters in need while refusing to give up hope for their own futures.

These are among the unheralded champions of Africa, the many people working to help their communities cope with loss. In this book, we offer their stories. Although most of the adults and children in the book are not infected with HIV themselves, all have been affected in some way by AIDS.

These people, with their grace and determination to move forward, touched us and stirred us to action. We hope their stories will move you to help them transform their hopes and dreams into reality.

– *Ruthann Richter & Karen Ande*
  August 2009

GOATS ARE A SALVATION FOR SOME FAMILIES, PROVIDING A SOURCE OF FOOD AND INCOME.

tales from tala

Joyce Nduku was cursed from the day she was born. Surely some ill spirit had looked down upon the child and her family. Or so her mother believed, for Joyce was disabled by cerebral palsy. When the baby was four months old, the mother headed for the bright lights of Nairobi and left the infant behind, wrapped in a blanket in the crossroads. The family would hear no news of the woman until years later, as she lay unconscious in a Nairobi hospital, dying of AIDS.

Joyce, 13, would have been a pariah in her rural village of Tala, Kenya, were it not for Monica Ngumi, a 4-foot-9 powerhouse of a woman. Ngumi has rescued many of the town's most vulnerable children—the orphaned and the handicapped—and offered them free schooling, meals and help with medical care, among other vital services.

"Before we started this program, the children were really suffering," Ngumi says. "They were very weak. Some could not carry anything. Most were malnourished. Now they are better off, and their health has improved."

A former teacher and administrator in the Nairobi slums, Ngumi settled in the 1990s in Tala, the ancestral home of her husband, Eliud Muema. The AIDS epidemic was going full bore, and the town was awash in orphans. "Everybody in town has been affected or infected. It's frightening," Ngumi says. She lost many relatives to the disease, including a niece, a sister-in-law and several cousins. Her beloved older sister, Mary, is HIV-positive. "It motivates me to work harder," she says.

With so many youngsters left adrift by the epidemic, Ngumi decided to mobilize the community to start a school. Muema, who managed a major Nairobi hotel until the post-9/11

JOYCE NDUKU AND A YOUNG FAMILY MEMBER

collapse in tourism, joined forces in the project. They named it in honor of their only daughter, Darlene, and evoking an African tradition that treasures motherhood, they called it Mama Darlene Children's Centre. The couple initially dug into their pockets for seed money and later learned how to apply for small grants from U.S. and European nonprofits. They branched out to provide HIV counseling. They formed a theatre troupe that combines entertaining skits with some serious prevention messages about HIV/AIDS. They also started a Goat Project, similar to the award-winning Heifer International, providing high-quality dairy goats to the most desperate families among them.

"Mama Darlene is a great example of the small things that can really change the world," says Natasha Martin, director of a California nonprofit who helped train Ngumi in organizational development.

The village of Tala is only an hour's drive from Nairobi, the raucous, urbane Kenyan capital, but it exists in a much slower time and place. In the morning, Ngumi buys her month's supply of beans in the village square—90 kilos in a burlap bag—which later arrives by ox-cart at the school a few hundred yards away.

RIGHT: MONICA NGUMI WITH ONE OF HER CHARGES

FACING PAGE: HER STUDENTS' EAGER FACES

The AIDS virus hitchhiked into Tala from the Kenyan capital with travelers on the two-lane highway, the town's only paved road. Local residents, many of whom have never ridden in a car, tread dirt paths through the scrub brush and the expanse of acacia trees to their mud huts, buried deep in the bush. Most are small farmers, growing maize, beans and vegetables in backyard gardens that barely sustain them and only when the rains cooperate.

We arrive in Tala—our first stop in Africa—bathed in the copper-colored dust of the dry season. Ngumi greets us with a handshake, the typical Kenyan welcome, and then wraps us in her strong embrace. She is of ample girth, with a broad face and sun-reddened cheeks. She has a throaty laugh and deep smile lines on her face. Sixty of her charges emerged from the cement-block school building, dressed in their red-checked uniforms. They raise their voices in welcome songs in Swahili and English: *Mungu akubariki sana...* God bless you much. Joyce stands in the front on her braced legs, arms held high in symbolic salute to the woman who gave her new life.

With Muema's guidance, we trek out into the bush to meet some of the many families who have benefited from Ngumi's energy and organizational talents. Our driver, a man in his 20s, takes us down a dirt path for about four miles until our ancient, junkyard Toyota can no longer negotiate the way through the stones and scrub. Our driver would be dead of AIDS just six months later. We walk a mile or so in the 90-degree Equatorial heat to a small, isolated collection of huts—the family compound for Ajuby Mutua, a gaunt-looking man in his early 50s, and his wife, Mary Nzula. Two of their grown daughters died within months of each other of AIDS, leaving behind 8-year-old cousins, Muani and Kamene. The grandparents took in the girls, though they couldn't afford to feed them on the grandfather's $2-a-day wage as a stonecutter in a nearby quarry. When the girls entered Ngumi's school, they were low in energy and spirits and had the reddish hair of *kwashiorkor*, a form of malnutrition.

The grandmother did not look well on that first visit, complaining of chest pain and lowering her head to rest it in her hands. She would later test positive for HIV and with Ngumi's help, obtain antiretroviral treatment, which started to become available in Tala in

2005. We saw her during our visit two years later, when she turned up at the school office, looking robust and cheerful. Her husband, meanwhile, had disappeared for several months and later returned, unwell himself. The grandmother now supports the family by selling bananas in town to riders on the *matatu*, the madcap Kenyan public taxi vans that shepherd people around the countryside.

On another adventure into the bush, we drive out to Joyce's house, a tiny stone hut with a gravel floor. Joyce was raised by her grandparents, farmers who survive by growing maize, beans and vegetables in their backyard. The rains passed them by this year. The crops are wilting in the field. "We miss the food," says her 74-year-old grandfather, John Nzioki. Tea suffices for breakfast. There is only one meal a day. It comes from family's stores of maize and beans from last year's crop. Joyce sleeps on dirty scraps of foam, as the family can't afford the $17 cost of a mattress.

ABOVE: NAP TIME

FACING PAGE: JOYCE AT HOME

TALES FROM TALA   **17**

METRO CAFE.

celtel
Making life better

NO POSTERS.

EASY 100/-
Top up now for 100/-

AVAILABLE HERE

TAKE AWAY CHIPS & SMOKIES

EGGS FOR

FACING PAGE: A DOWNTOWN CAFE

RIGHT: CHILDREN PLAY ON A VELVETEEN COUCH THAT RESIDENTS CARRIED INTO THE COURTYARD TO ACCOMMODATE THEIR AMERICAN GUESTS.

For the first five years of her life, Joyce made her way around town in the arms of her grandfather, who dotes on the young girl. Ngumi then arranged for her to have surgery at a mission hospital to release the taut tendons in her legs so she could walk. Today, she negotiates the five miles to school every day on her own. Without the school's help, "she would be a neglected child. She would not even be considered somebody," Ngumi says. Joyce's outgoing nature has won her many friends at school. She has made progress in basic subjects.

"People were wondering, how could she learn?" her grandfather says. "Later the people ask, 'Is it the same girl?' They can't believe it now because she is in such good condition." He smiles broadly. He has few teeth remaining.

Ngumi has expanded the school from four to six classrooms, using a grant from the Firelight Foundation in Santa Cruz, Calif. Some 160 children now attend the school, housed in bright blue and green buildings. "I want the children to have great futures," Ngumi says. Tragically, Ngumi died of liver cancer in February 2007; nearly 1,000 people mourned her passing at the day-long funeral service. Muema and his children, including daughter Darlene, now carry on her legacy.

CHILDREN IN SCHOOL, STUDYING THE CAMERA

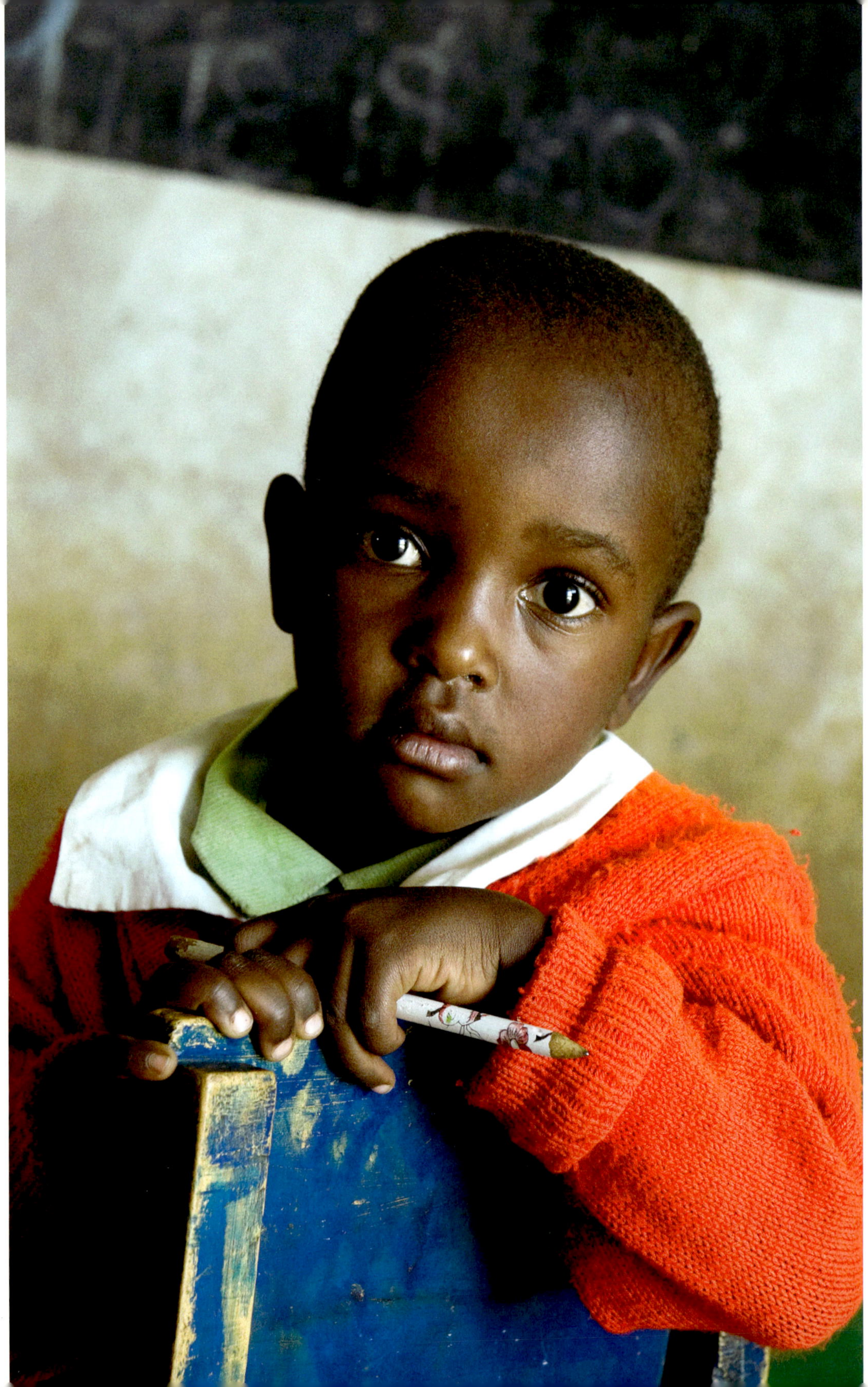

LEFT: A STUDENT AT
MAMA DARLENE

FACING PAGE: ROSE, ONE OF
SIX HANDICAPPED CHILDREN
IN A FAMILY, HAD SEVERAL
OPERATIONS TO HELP
STRAIGHTEN HER BOWED LEGS.

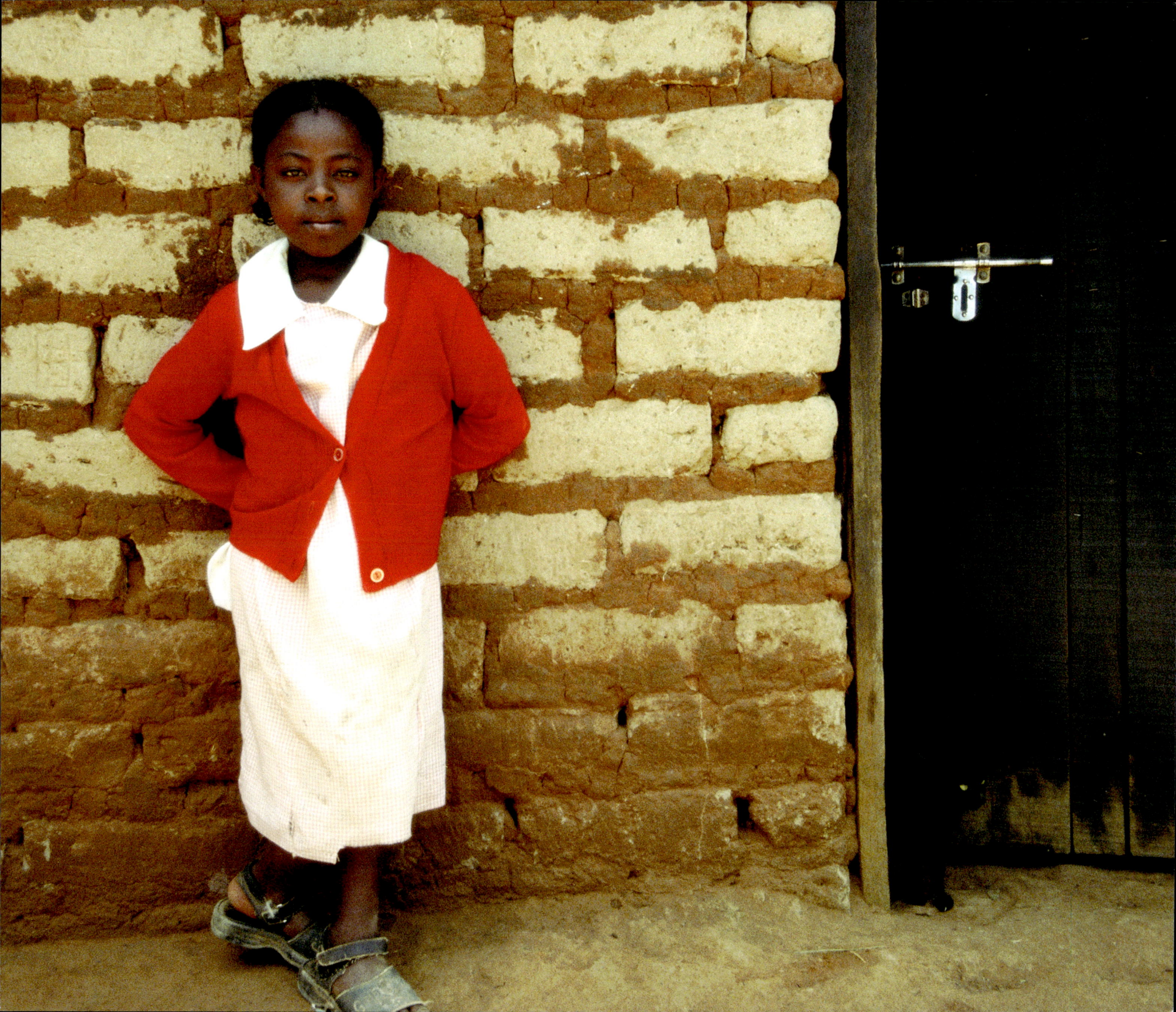

gilgil: the survivors

Two-year-old Mary Maishon was near death when she was found with two other children living under a piece of cardboard and plastic. Her limbs were skeletal, bent from lack of nutrition, and she was barely able to sit up. She didn't speak at all.

Mary had been living with her 4-year-old sister, Caroline, and 3-year-old cousin, Kevin, in a run-down section of Gilgil, a farming community in Kenya's Rift Valley highlands. At night, the children slept half-naked on a urine-soaked blanket on the chilly earth. The three had been left in the care of their grandfather after their parents died of AIDS, but the grandfather was an alcoholic who was rarely home.

"When we arrived on foot—there are no roads there—the kids were scared and scuttled inside the shack crying," recalls Jill Simpson, a retired nurse who had been called in to help. "I followed and tripped over a bundle of rags that moved and cried weakly—Mary."

Simpson brought the children to the Saidia Children's Home, a shelter for children she founded in 2004. Saidia, which means "help" in Swahili, began as a modest undertaking with just two children in a decaying building. Now it is a large, well-established project, occupying a new, two-story home that is positively luxurious by local standards. It serves as a place of last resort for the town's neglected and abandoned youngsters, including many whose parents have been lost to AIDS.

The project got its impetus from a local businesswoman, Jane Kinuthia, who had been feeding some of Gilgil's street children at her downtown café. Kinuthia realized they needed more help than she could provide, for the number of these homeless children was rapidly growing. She also was

MARY MAISHON

besieged by aging grannies who were hard-pressed to care for their orphaned grandchildren. One Sunday at church she issued a plea to the congregation.

"We need help from the community—maize and beans for the children, because they are crying," she said. "The women are coming to me, crying too—grannies with young children. They have been coming—many of them." She also appealed to Simpson, now 78, a longtime children's advocate who had already founded one orphanage in the neighboring town of Naivasha. Simpson had worked in the mobile health centers of the Flying Doctors, an air ambulance service run by the African Medical and Research Foundation, and had started a string of polio clinics for children. She had even once trekked on camelback in the desolate, bandit-ridden plains around Lake Turkana in northern Kenya as a fundraiser, bringing in more than $38,000 for a home for handicapped youngsters—an absolute fortune by Kenyan standards. But the orphan problem in Gilgil was beyond anything she had encountered before.

"We were paying school fees for some of the children or collecting money to help them with clothing and food. But then we realized it's

LEFT: JANE KINUTHIA IN THE NEW BUILDING DURING CONSTRUCTION

FACING PAGE: THE LINE FOR MORNING TEA

more than that: So many of these children have mothers who are dying," she says. "These children have nowhere to go, and the grannies can't cope. That made me push to find something."

Simpson launched Saidia in a rented cement-block building Kinuthia had once used for her catering business. Kinuthia and social worker Teresa Wahito now manage the home, where the children get three meals a day, generous fare in a country where a meal a day is often the norm. The youngest children at the shelter attend an on-site nursery school, while the older ones benefit from sponsorships to attend private schools in the community.

The orphanage began with two children, but was soon overwhelmed by demand. It now houses nearly 50 youngsters, including some young refugees from the violence following the 2007 elections in which members of the opposition took to the streets to protest what it claimed were rigged elections by the incumbent party.

ABOVE: JILL SIMPSON

RIGHT: PRE-SCHOOL AT THE ORPHANAGE

GILGIL: THE SURVIVORS   31

The numbers would grow after Simpson and Kinuthia stumbled upon a rag-tag group of children living in a particularly gritty part of town. The row of shacks was occupied by commercial sex workers—Gilgil's equivalent of a red-light district. While the women entertained clients for about $1 per encounter, their young charges hid under the beds or romped in the dirt outside.

Here Kinuthia first encountered Demaris Muthoni, who was nearly four years old but was as tiny and frail as a newborn, weighing less than 10 pounds. "I had to put her on my shoulder, she was so weak," she recalls. "In all my years in Gilgil, I had never seen anything like this."

Demaris had been slowly starving to death in the care of her 17-year-old aunt, Carol, who was an orphan herself. When Demaris' mother died of AIDS, she entrusted her two little girls to Carol's care. But Carol, whose mother was a commercial sex worker, had never been to school, so she turned to the only work she had ever known.

"When I was left with the orphans, I was jobless," Carol says in Swahili. "The children slept hungry for several days, and there was

FACING PAGE: DEMARIS MUTHONI

RIGHT: CHILDREN IN THE RED-LIGHT DISTRICT

nothing else I could do." She is wearing blue jeans and a sweatshirt and has a pretty round face, framed by corn rows. Her eyes have a glazed look, and she is having trouble walking straight, as she has been filling her empty stomach with the illegal alcoholic brew, changaa, that she sells to her clients. Carol says she doesn't know if she is HIV-positive, one of the dangerous side-effects of her profession, but she doesn't want to find out.

The discovery of Demaris and her little companions spawned another project for Saidia's founders: a satellite nursery school and nutrition program. They fixed up a ramshackle building in the neighborhood, added a corrugated iron roof and hired a teacher to run the school on the second floor. They also began feeding the children using funds from a small grant and food donations from the community.

"I don't know that there is any hope for these women, but there is hope yet for the children," Simpson says.

Simpson also raised $120,000, much of it from friends in England and the United States, to build a new, 6,000-square-foot permanent home for Saidia that opened in January 2008. The building has two large dormitories, one each for the boys and girls, and rare amenities such as tiled bathrooms with indoor toilets and solar panels to provide light so the children can do homework at night.

Both Demaris and Mary have made themselves comfortably at home there. Demaris is now basking in her regular meals, her warm bed and her hand-me-down dresses. She is slowly regaining her health and energy. "She is a very good-natured child and likes to be clean and tidy," Kinuthia says while Demaris plays catch outside.

Mary, who learned to stand up with the help of a walker, is now a mischievous child who runs through the corridors, telling stories and relating bits of news. She and her sister, Caroline, "take life very seriously but, I am delighted to say, they are normal and naughty children," Simpson says. Mary still dreams of the day when her absent grandfather will come and bring her sweets and hold her hand, but the dream comes far less often now.

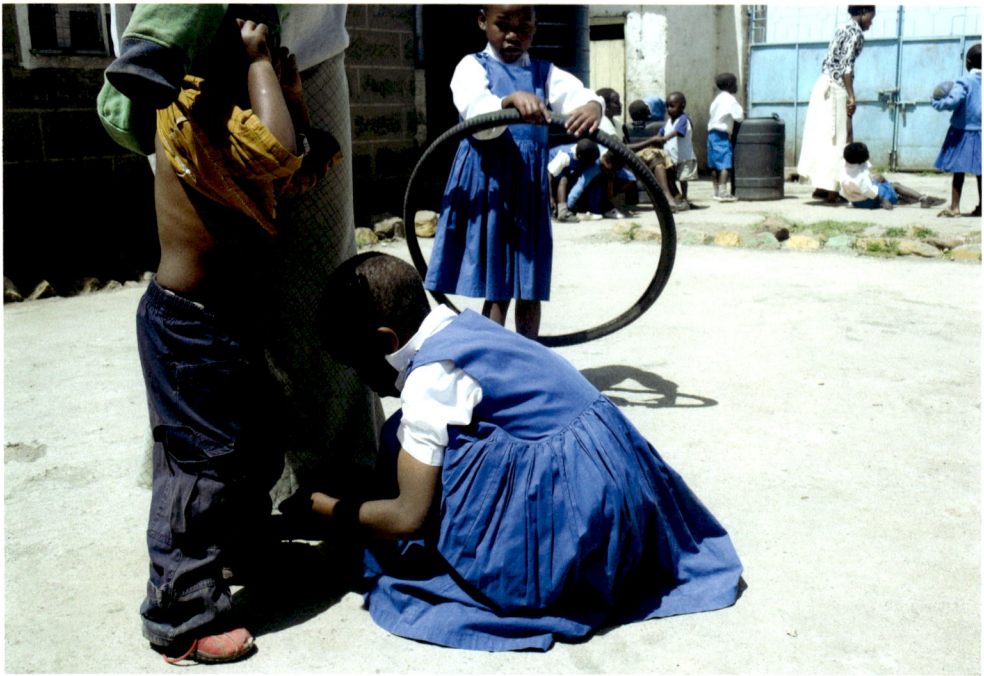

ABOVE: IN THE PLAYGROUND

FACING PAGE: MARY SNACKS ON A BANANA.

ABOVE: IT WAS WEEKS BEFORE KEVIN WAIHARO COULD BE PARTED FROM HIS PLAID GREEN JACKET, A GIFT FROM THE MAN HE CALLED "DADDY." DADDY HAD RESCUED KEVIN AFTER HIS MOTHER WAS MURDERED, BRINGING THE BOY TO A HOTEL ROOM IN GILGIL. DADDY DIED OF AIDS, BUT KEVIN CONTINUED TO WEAR THE GREEN COAT IN THE HOPE THAT HE WOULD RETURN SOMEDAY. THE COAT IS OFF NOW, AND KEVIN HAS SETTLED INTO HIS NEW HOME AT SAIDIA (RIGHT).

GILGIL: THE SURVIVORS 37

A GAME OF HIDE AND SEEK

esther's world

We head down an unmarked dirt road to the home of Susan Andukais, who is entombed on a makeshift wooden bed, the only furniture in the tin shanty. It is mid-day, yet only stray bits of light enter through the single window and the pockmarked walls of the shack in the Rift Valley town of Naivasha.

Susan is in the last throes of AIDS, with the unrelenting cough of AIDS-related tuberculosis. It takes all of her energy to lift her head in greeting, but she does so out of respect for her American guests. We shake hands in the typical Kenyan welcome, but her grasp is barely there; at 34, she is a skeleton of a person, her shrunken face marred by grief.

Susan says she fell ill six months before our visit in March 2004 and had to give up her living as a cattle-tender. Now all responsibility for the family falls to 13-year-old Esther, the oldest child, who cares for her dying mother, as well as the three younger boys in the family.

"When I first came to the home, it really touched me. Actually, it horrified me," says Teresa Wahito, the community social worker who has brought us to meet the family.

Esther stoops to light some bits of charcoal in the corner to prepare the family's only meal of the day—a lunch of *ugali*, a corn meal mush, and some cabbage. She is barefoot, neatly dressed in a lavender top and skirt. Her short-cropped hair has the reddish tinge of *kwashiorkor*, a form of malnutrition. She moves with remarkable grace and does not complain.

"When I see my mother sick, I feel bad," she says softly in Swahili. "When I find there is no food, I don't know what to do."

ESTHER IPECHE

Esther could be the poster child of the epidemic, one of hundreds of thousands of youngsters who have lost their childhood to AIDS. Were it not for the disease, she might be going to school and tittering in the yard with her friends. But as the head of the family now, she has more urgent responsibilities: She needs to find food for a meal, to help feed and dress her mother and to keep her little brothers safe.

We leave Esther in a somber mood, for we realize her mother is not long for this world. Soon the four children will have to find their way on their own.

The next time we visit Esther, it's a year-and-a-half later, and her circumstances are remarkably changed. She and her brothers have found refuge in the Saidia Children's Home in Gilgil, about an hour's drive north of Naivasha.

Orphanages are generally discouraged in the AIDS care community as a first response to the needs of orphans. This is because studies show that children grow best in supportive families and don't always thrive in an institutional environment. The better alternative, children's advocates say, is to shore up traditional community and family networks so they can embrace youngsters who have lost their parents.

RIGHT: ESTHER AND HER BROTHER, KANYARI

FACING PAGE: ESTHER'S YOUNGEST BROTHER, PATRICK, WITH THEIR MOTHER, SUSAN, THREE WEEKS BEFORE SUSAN'S DEATH

ESTHER'S WORLD 43

Unfortunately for some children, this is not a possibility. The nuns in Naivasha searched for months for a family who would take in Esther and her brothers. No one came forward because the community is so taxed by disease and poverty. So if it were not for Saidia, the children would have nowhere to go.

Esther now is the oldest child at the shelter, surrounded by a sprawling brood of youngsters who spill out of the doorways. She seems to be content, playing the role of mother hen for this raucous collection of once-neglected and abandoned children. She hangs up laundry, wipes a child's running rose and soothes a chubby child known only as "Baby," the latest arrival.

Esther's oldest brother Kanyari, 9, is gleefully lobbing a donated soccer ball in the courtyard with another boy. He has weathered a long bout with tuberculosis, which he may have contracted from his mother, and is no longer lacking for energy. He has a mischievous smile and loves mugging for the camera. The youngest brother, Patrick, 5, who I remember as a sad, doe-eyed boy, is said to be among the brightest of the children, rich in academic promise.

LEFT: KANYARI LOBS A SOCCER BALL

FACING PAGE: ESTHER'S YOUNGEST BROTHER, PATRICK, AT SAIDIA ORPHANAGE

Esther is attending public school now for the first time, assigned to the second grade, with students more than half her age and size. She endures the ridicule of her younger classmates for the sake of an education. She's learning to do sums and to read and write in both Swahili and English. The teacher has entrusted her with the keys to the school, with the responsibility of locking up at the end of the day.

Esther is 15 now and considering her options for the future. She says she would like to learn a trade, such as hairdressing or sewing, something on which she can depend for a livelihood.

"She's safe and sound now," says Jill Simpson, the orphanage founder. "She's got three meals a day and is well-cared for. But what's the next step? That's the worry. It's a step into the unknown."

ABOVE AND RIGHT: ESTHER AND HER BROTHERS
SHORTLY BEFORE THEIR MOTHER'S DEATH

CAPTION

Two years later, the answer arrives in part in an envelope. Esther, now a shy 17-year-old with a reasonable command of English, has been accepted to a program in Nairobi in which she will be schooled in the art of tailoring. She will be in a class of 200 boys and girls who have been selected from among 10,000 applicants. She receives the letter with a mix of excitement and trepidation, for it means she will be heading to the city on her own, leaving her brothers behind. She prepares for her new assignment with a visit to a local store with her American friends to buy new shoes, as her only pair is worn through.

She heads to Nairobi with modest ambitions: "I just want to be a good person," she says. Today, Esther has some precious assets: a sewing machine and the skill to set out on her own independent path.

ESTHER AT SAIDIA, SHORTLY BEFORE HER DEPARTURE
FOR TAILORING SCHOOL IN NAIROBI

priestly blessings

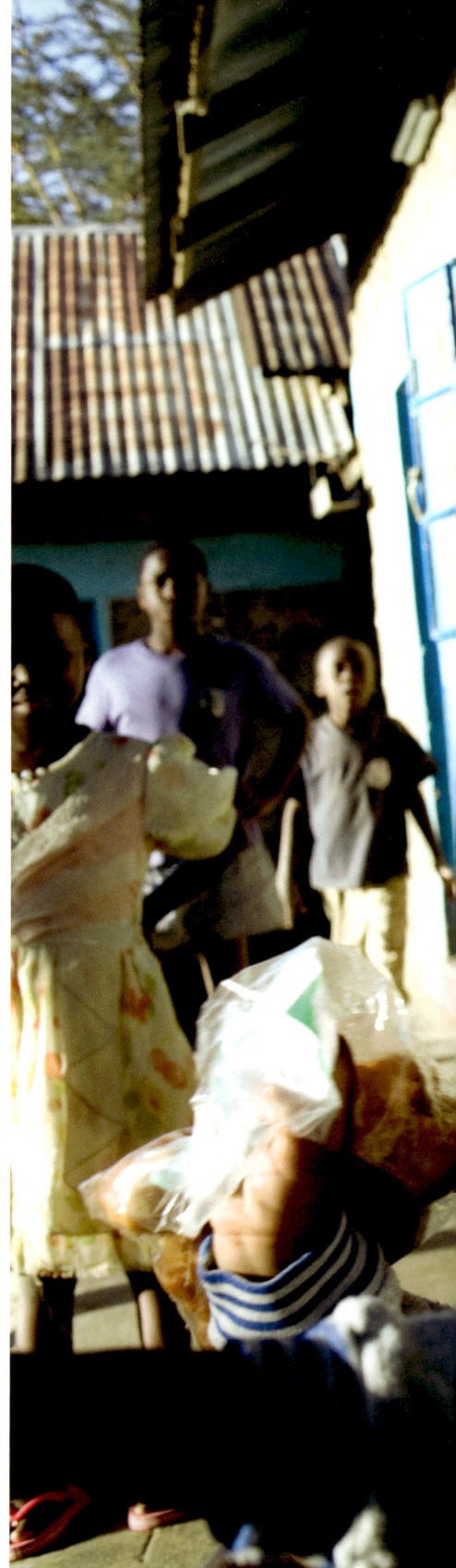

Some 30 women, dressed in modest skirts and blouses, gather in a circle with Father Daniel Kiriti, the parish priest in Naivasha, laughing and crying about the challenges of their profession and their daily lives. They are (or were) commercial sex workers. All are single mothers who took to the streets to help feed their children. Today, they are sharing some of their most embarrassing moments, intimate stories often relating to sexual encounters gone awry.

The women are also peer counselors and educators for LifeBloom Services International, a U.S.-sponsored nonprofit that aims to help these Kenyan women, some of whom are HIV-positive, find alternatives to a risky life on the streets.

These women say they have been shunned by the community and by members of the church because of their profession. The priest has reached out and supported them as they work to make the difficult transition. One of the women, Nancy, stands up at the close of the two-hour support group meeting and addresses the priest, tears in her eyes.

"You were the one who took us in first and accepted us and showed us we're just like other people," she says as the women all clap and nod in unison. Because of the priest's outreach in the community, she says, she can now enter the church and pray with her head held high. Another member of the group thanks the priest for bringing the women together and teaching them about condom use. "Otherwise we would be dead of AIDS," she says, and no one would be left to care for their children.

In his five years in Naivasha, Father Kiriti, 48, has become a powerful influence in the community and an activist in the fight against HIV/AIDS. He ministers to a population of some

FATHER KIRITI AND TOLEO, AGE TWO

250,000 people, many of them poor rural farmers, in a region brought low by the disease.

"A week without a funeral is a good week," the priest says somberly.

Naivasha is best known for its lake of thousands of flamingos and its lavish lakeside hotels that draw tourists from around the world. But it is also home to a large number of migrants who have come seeking work in the local flower industry. They live in slums that are rife with AIDS and other diseases. AIDS also has flourished locally as a result of Kenya's tribal clashes over the course of the last decade, in which families have suffered the trauma of home and job loss, dislocation and separation.

The son of a poor Kenyan farmer, Kiriti is a short, slender man with dark chocolate skin, short-cropped graying hair and a deep, powerful voice that resonates in the church. He typically dresses in Nike sneakers and polo shirts, which he prefers over the traditional Roman Catholic collar because it puts him closer to the people, he says. When he was ordained in 1988, he says he never envisioned he would one day be trying to stem a pandemic.

ABOVE: LAKE NAIVASHA

LEFT: RITA, WHO SPRANG BACK TO LIFE AFTER OBTAINING
ANTIRETROVIRAL DRUGS WITH THE CHURCH'S HELP

PRIESTLY BLESSINGS   53

"I knew from the moment I entered the priesthood that I would become a people's advocate. I would stand for the people—be a voice for the voiceless," he says. "But who knew about AIDS then?"

Today, he actively preaches HIV prevention to his flock, exhorting the thousands who attend Mass on Sunday to go for HIV testing and to change their behavior to prevent the spread of the disease. Privately he advises young people on condom use, though it's not officially condoned by the church.

"I encourage people to know their alternatives. Science is here to help us, to complement our faith," he says.

His AIDS work also has become intensely personal. In 2005, his sister-in-law became critically ill with HIV-related complications and was unconscious, near death. With the aid of antiretroviral treatment, she literally rose from her hospital bed and is doing well today. Her HIV-positive husband—Kiriti's brother—is also receiving treatment, as is their five-year-old son, who suffers intermittent health problems.

"For me, AIDS is not out there. It's here," the priest says, gently placing his hand on his heart, "in a very painful way."

LEFT AND FACING PAGE: PEER EDUCATORS WITH LIFEBLOOM SERVICES INTERNATIONAL HELP OUT BY SHINING SHOES AT THE CHURCH ORPHANAGE.

Kiriti has taken a special interest in the children who have lost parents to the disease, overseeing an orphanage for 35 children on the church grounds. Most are children who have been abandoned, neglected or abused and don't have living relatives able to care for them. The youngest member of the group, Toleo, was left in a paper bag on the parish fence. She was hours old, still bathed in her mother's fluids. The parishioner who found her brought her to the priest's door early one Sunday morning.

"I was in shock," the priest says. "But the immediate thought that came to me was the health of the child."

As he feared, the baby tested HIV-positive. The priest named her Toleo, Swahili for "offertory," for he'd first mistaken the paper bag as an offering to the church. Today, Toleo shares a closet-sized

ABOVE: AN ART PROJECT AT THE ORPHANAGE

RIGHT: MICHAEL, A CHILD AT THE ORPHANAGE WHO WAS ABANDONED AS AN INFANT

room with the housemother at the orphanage. She no longer has evidence of the virus in her system and is a healthy, 4-year-old, a shining little girl who has captured Kiriti's heart.

The priest says he worries about the future of children such as Toleo, for only with good education can they succeed in life. So he has led a campaign to build the first high school in Naivasha devoted exclusively to training young girls. With help from donors in the United States and Europe, the school opened to its first pupils in February 2007. In January 2009, it welcomed another 70 students, doubling the school population.

"For me, education is a keynote because it helps empower both girls and boys as they encounter difficult forces in life," he says. "One of the enemies is AIDS. With education, we can teach them how to protect themselves and how to address the issue of AIDS in their lives."

LEFT: FATHER KIRITI WITH TOLEO, ONE MONTH AFTER SHE WAS FOUND

FACING PAGE: KIDS RACE TO SUNDAY MASS.

LEFT: A YOUNG WOMAN, ONE OF MORE THAN 1,800 HIV-POSITIVE INDIVIDUALS WHO ATTEND CHURCH-SPONSORED SUPPORT GROUPS

FACING PAGE: CHILDREN AT THE ORPHANAGE

kibera: nairobi's underbelly

One of Janet Nyaboke's few possessions—and the one she cherishes above all—is a book of 3-by-5 photos that opens to her mother's obituary from the local newspaper. The frayed, yellowed clipping shows a somber-looking woman and lists the numerous members of her extended family who have all passed on. But the story doesn't begin to capture the impact of her death from AIDS just two months before, for it left Janet feeling utterly alone. At age 15, she is struggling to stay in school while managing a little fruit and vegetable stand to earn income for rent and food for herself and her little brother. "When I start thinking about mother," she says, "I start singing and praising God to save me from my sorrows."

Janet lives in a spare, dark room of about 100 square feet in Kibera, the notorious slum on the edge of the Kenyan capital of Nairobi. It is one of the world's largest slums with a million people wedged tightly together in a sea of tin-roofed shanties that stretch over a square mile. In late 2007, it was a flashpoint for Kenya's post-election violence, as groups from rival tribes clashed in the streets and set entire neighborhoods on fire.

Kibera is a maze of rocky, garbage-strewn alleyways with no sanitation or water system and electrical service that is spotty at best. We trip over rivulets of sewage and mud in these rugged back-alley streets, where children romp and residents hang their clothes to dry, as personal hygiene is still prized in this otherwise gritty environment.

The neighborhood is fertile territory for AIDS. While the prevalence of the virus among Kenya's adults has declined to 6.7 percent nationwide, it has remained higher in Kibera, where more than 11 percent are infected, according to 2007 figures from Kenya's National AIDS Control Council.

AN AERIAL VIEW OF KIBERA

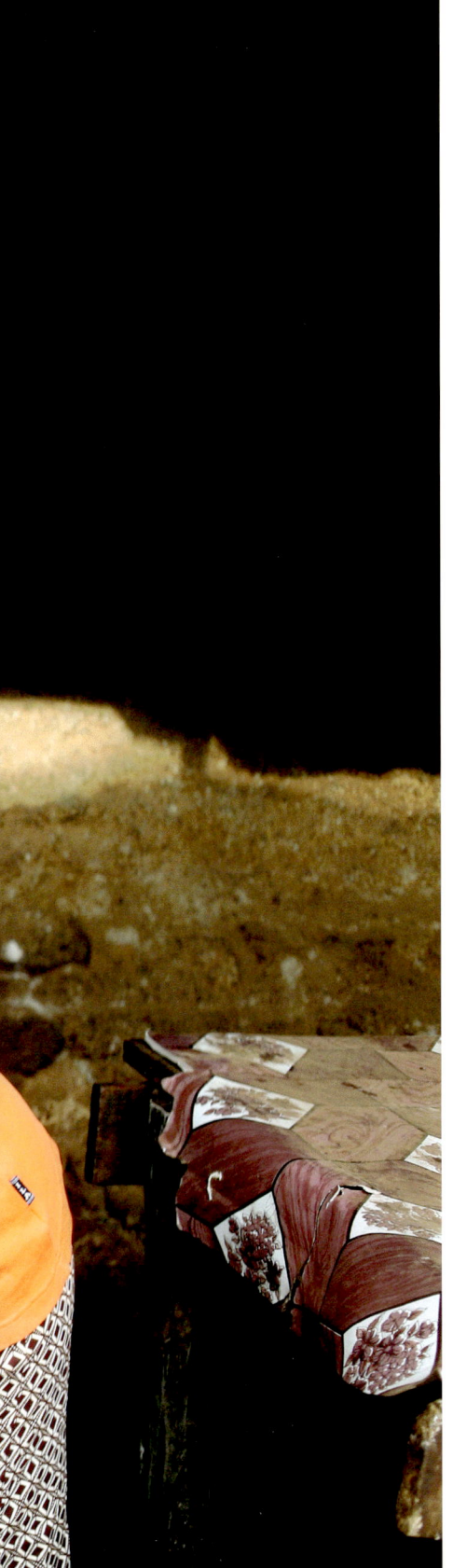

Kibera is also home to many community-based organizations that have risen up to fight the disease. Among these is Kibera Hamlets, a nonprofit that aims to empower young women, provide HIV counseling and disseminate information about HIV/AIDS through a theatre program that both educates and entertains. Their Girl Power program offers emotional and practical support, such as food and rent, to orphaned teens like Janet who could easily slide into a life of prostitution or petty crime without outside support.

"If there is no one who stands for these girls, then they are finished. If they don't get good guidance, they end up on the streets because no one can provide for them," says John Adoli, a former soccer player who is founder and director of the group. "But if someone comes in for them, they feel they can do something and move forward."

ABOVE: JOHN ADOLI

LEFT: JANET NYABOKE AT HER FRUIT STAND

KIBERA: NAIROBI'S UNDERBELLY

Among those the group has supported are Yvonne Amale and Jackline Achieng, two teenagers who have lost their childhood to AIDS. Orphans who also serve as sole caregivers for younger brothers and sisters, they are part of a burgeoning new category in the AIDS lexicon—the child-headed family—of which there are many thousands in sub-Saharan Africa.

Yvonne was only 12 when her parents died, and her sister, Tina, was a newborn. Yvonne missed a year of school to nurse her bedridden mother and father, who suffered from a succession of ailments—tuberculosis, malaria, diarrhea, fevers. "I was worried, but I tried my best," she says. She did the washing and cooking and stayed at their side in their last days. "They told me I should keep care of my little sister and give her some guidance. They told me I should not be with bad friends," Yvonne says during a break in her studies at school.

She is a slender girl, neatly dressed in her blue school uniform skirt and sweater, with a round face, bright smile and soft but determined voice. After class, she sells sweets on the street for a few shillings to earn a bit of income, and she and her sister survive mostly on fried kale, the cheapest source of food

RIGHT: YVONNE AMALE AND HER SISTER, TINA

FACING PAGE: JACKLINE ACHIENG AND SIBLINGS

KIBERA: NAIROBI'S UNDERBELLY **67**

available. Kibera Hamlets has worked with her landlord to see that she and Tina aren't tossed onto the street. Their tidy house of mud and sticks, next to a pile of rusted tin and rubble, is hardly big enough to hold a bed, a wooden table and two stools, but it is filled with signs of hope—magazine pages with pictures of luxury homes and pretty landscapes. While Yvonne is away at school, neighbors watch over Tina, who is almost two. No amount of effort from her American visitors can coax a smile from the little girl, who disappears behind a hanging sheet to munch privately on a gift of cashews and a protein bar.

When Yvonne was in the 8th grade, she pleaded with school officials to let her continue her education, though she didn't have the U.S. equivalent of $5 for her school fees. Kibera Hamlets has helped find people willing to sponsor the education of her and other girls. Yvonne's big wish is to be able to stay through high school and beyond: "I want to become a nurse so I can help the sick," she says.

ABOVE: CHILDREN AT PLAY IN THE STREET

LEFT: A BACK ALLEY IN KIBERA

KIBERA: NAIROBI'S UNDERBELLY 69

Yvonne's ailing parents might have lived, had they gone earlier to one of several clinics in Kibera which now dispense antiretroviral drugs free of charge, Adoli says. But they waited too long to make the trip there, fearing that stigma would taint the family's reputation.

"One of the big problems we have in Kibera is that if someone is infected, he or she just wants to keep it alone," Adoli says. "If they tell people, neighbors won't want to associate with their family. So they fear they will be isolated or their families will be isolated. So they don't seek treatment. That is how stigma kills."

So it was, too, with Jackline, 15, whose home off a steep, rocky alley is just steps away from a three-room health clinic. Her parents, both tailors who died within a month of each other, were too ashamed to visit the clinic, even though they could have received free treatment there for the AIDS-related infections that plagued them. After their deaths in 2005, Jackline's uncle disowned her, for he wanted nothing to do with disease, she says. So at age 13, she found herself with four brothers and sisters to care for by herself.

"I was somewhat confused," she says, "but there was nothing I could do."

LEFT: A THREE-PLATE LUNCH

FACING PAGE: ONE OF OUR GUIDES IN KIBERA

She has a pretty, triangular-shaped face framed by a purple scarf, which she uses to cover her head, freshly shaved to discourage lice. She dropped out of her 8th-grade class to care for her siblings; two of them, Blessing, 5 and Felix, 6, play outside in the alley, which is filled with refuse and discarded plastic bags. Jackline sells kale, bananas and tomatoes in the market and hopes to cobble together the $5 she needs to take her exams so she can move on with her education. "I hope to be a teacher," she says, "because I like teachers." She has no time for self-pity. "I just accept the reality."

ABOVE: KIBERA HAMLETS HELPS VANNAH, 15, WHO HAS FIVE YOUNGER BROTHERS AND SISTERS TO LOOK AFTER.

RIGHT: WILLARD, A BOARD MEMBER OF KIBERA HAMLETS

KIBERA: NAIROBI'S UNDERBELLY **73**

ABOVE: DANCING SCHOOLGIRLS IN KIBERA

LEFT: PRIMARY SCHOOL STUDENTS, KIBERA HAMLETS

ABOVE: FRIENDS AT SCHOOL

FACING PAGE: BLESSING (CENTER) AND FELIX (RIGHT),
JACKLINE ACHIENG'S YOUNGER SISTER AND BROTHER

growing up with hiv

Like a student eager to be first in line, 12-year-old William Mmemba bounds out to greet us on his stick-thin legs. He has a long face and a head too large for a body that stopped growing several years ago. That is when he fell ill with tuberculosis and tests at the nearby government hospital in Naivasha showed he was infected with HIV.

"He was so weak, he could not shake my hand," says Jecinta Gakahu, the community social worker who has accompanied us to his home. William, who lost his mother to AIDS-related meningitis in 2005, is now being raised by his father, Joseph Mbsa, 30, who was fired from his job as a food service worker when his HIV-positive status became known.

William is among the estimated 140,000 children in Kenya—and one of 2.3 million in sub-Saharan Africa—who are living with HIV. Most of these children contracted the virus from their infected mothers at birth or during breast-feeding. Sixty to 70 percent die by their fifth birthday. But in some children, such as William, the disease progresses slowly, and they may do well, provided they get proper medical treatment and support, says Dr. Helena Huerga, the medical coordinator in Nairobi for the Geneva-based Doctors Without Borders.

Both William and his father are taking antiretroviral drugs which they obtain free of charge from Kijabe Hospital near Naivasha, which receives some support from U.S.-based organizations such as Project CURE and the Elizabeth Glaser Pediatric AIDS Foundation. Anti-AIDS drugs specifically formulated for children were late in coming to Africa, becoming available in Kenya in early 2006. Now William and thousands of other youngsters are benefiting from these medications. William's

JOSEPH MBSA PLAYS WITH HIS SON, WILLIAM.

CD4 count, a measure of key infection-fighting cells in his immune system, has increased, and he's stronger today, able to grip my hand.

But the treatment, which requires him to take 16 pills everyday, may have come too late. The virus has entered his brain, and he suffers from seizures. He has some brain damage as a result and when asked a question, he thinks long and hard about the answer, which is often just a "yes" or "no." He says English is his favorite subject in school, though when he recites a poem he's learned, it comes out as gibberish.

"I'm talking with him, but I see it's affecting his mind," says his father, a remarkably cheerful man who is freshly showered and ready for church this Sunday morning. If William's schoolmates knew he was HIV-positive, the father says, they would likely scorn him, for children often suffer socially because of the disease.

ABOVE: JOSEPH AT HOME

RIGHT: JOSEPH WITH WILLIAM

Kevin, 17, another HIV-positive youngster from Nairobi, says he was shunned by his classmates because of his ailment.

"When I was in class 4 (the fourth grade), the children were quarreling with me because I had rashes on my face," says the teen, who is now in the 8th grade. "They would not sit with me."

On a separate visit, we meet Kevin and four other children affected by HIV/AIDS outside Leototo Kibera, a community-based care program in the Nairobi slum that is devoted to children with the disease.

Kevin, a friendly boy who's eager to shake our hand, is wearing glasses and has the shuffling manner of an awkward teen. When he was 12, he fell ill with a spate of problems: tuberculosis, herpes, meningitis and a skin rash that covered his body. He lost hearing in one ear and suffered some brain damage as a result of the meningitis, which has slowed his progress in school. He is now trying to catch up on the work he missed because of his illnesses, and has managed to make some new friends.

His mother, Mary, says she found out she was HIV-positive in 1997 when she was pregnant with her second child, Kevin's younger

FACING PAGE: KEVIN BRAIDS HIS MOTHER'S HAIR.

RIGHT: BEAD MAKING

brother. Her husband was very sick as well and died shortly thereafter of AIDS-related tuberculosis.

"I was very stressed and had many worries of how I would look after my children," Mary says. "My health deteriorated where I had to be carried to the hospital."

She now supports the family through her work as a hairdresser, a business she started with a help of a California-based nonprofit called the Village Enterprise Fund. The fund provides small grants to the desperately poor in East Africa to help them start life-sustaining businesses. Kevin, who fashioned his mother's hair that day with several dyed and braided strands, says he'd like to be hairdresser himself or maybe an electrician. "I like to operate the wires," he says.

While Kevin comes forward to meet us during our visit to Leototo Kibera, another boy in the group, 9-year-old Michael, hangs back from the conversation and bows his head when approached. He is a very slender child, wearing a faded blue sweater with the logo of the San Francisco 49ers football team. He is low on energy because of a history of anemia, among other health problems, says his mother, Evelyn Alvnyola.

Alvnyola, 33, learned she was HIV-positive after she lost a son in infancy. The diagnosis came as a huge blow, for she had five children to care for, including two she had inherited from an aunt who passed on.

"I was so sad because I had told her I would take care of her kids. In that moment, I discovered my own (HIV) status. So I felt sorry because I felt my life was reached to the end, and yet I had two other children to take care of. They had no mother or father. I was their mother and father," she says.

Her husband, also sick, lost his job, and the landlord evicted the family from their home, tossing their few belongings into the street.

"We had nothing," she says. "We were as orphans. We were just blind."

With help from the Village Enterprise Fund, Alvnyola bought a sewing machine and now makes school uniforms for sale. On her own initiative, she also began a small enterprise making soap and beaded necklaces to supplement the family's income.

Michael, who is now in kindergarten, is now receiving antiretroviral treatment, and his health has improved. His mother has not given up hope.

EVELYN ALVNYOLA AND HER SON, MICHAEL

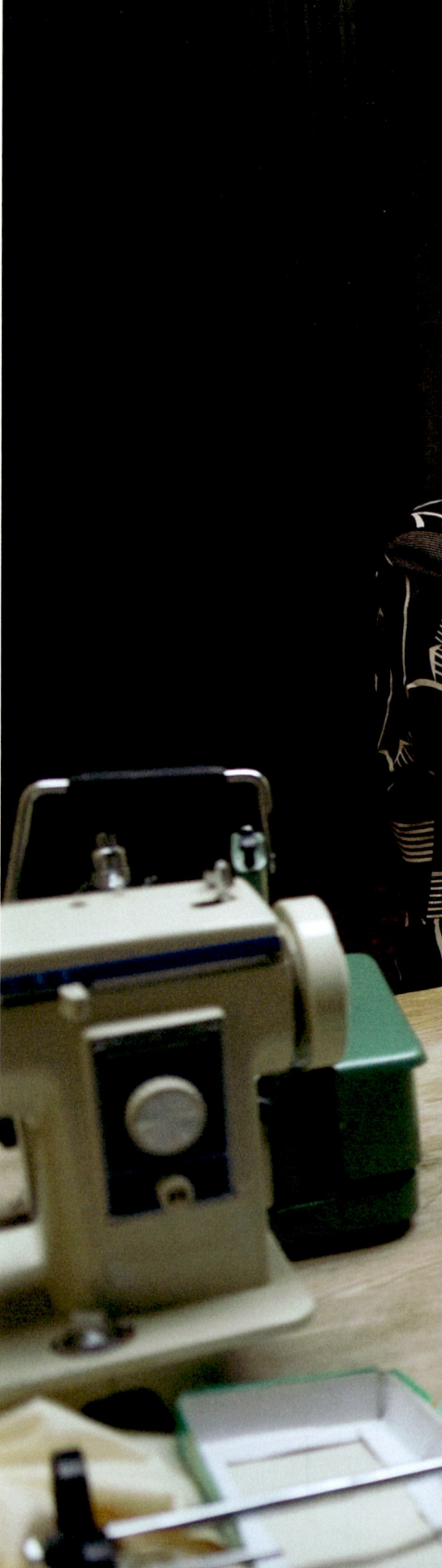

Kenya began a program in 2004 that could have spared Michael his suffering. Because most children acquire HIV at birth, the authorities now offer pregnant women testing for the virus. Those who test positive may choose to be treated with antiretroviral drugs before and during delivery; their babies get the medication just after birth. In the United States, this strategy has reduced the number of HIV-infected babies to near zero.

Susan Kimani, a 36-year-old, unemployed Protestant minister from the city of Nakuru, is among those who have benefited from the new program. She says she lived in fear for years that she

ABOVE AND RIGHT: EVELYN AND A GROUP OF HIV-POSITIVE WOMEN DESIGN SCHOOL UNIFORMS IN A PROJECT SUPPORTED BY THE VILLAGE ENTERPRISE FUND.

might be HIV-positive because she had not been feeling well for so long. She married in 2003 and four years later became pregnant with the couple's first child. She decided to go for HIV testing for the sake of the baby, she says. She came to Naivasha, where she could receive medical care at the government hospital, moving into the modest home of her sister.

"I feared my child would die," she says, close to tears. After she tested positive, she agonized over how to tell her husband, who initially took the news in silence. He disappeared a week later. Kimani began antiretroviral treatment a month before her delivery. To her great relief, she gave birth to a healthy girl in October 2007.

SUSAN KIMANI (FAR LEFT) WITH
A COMMUNITY HEALTH WORKER

go go grannies: africa's well of hope

Sara Nduku, a revered member of her Kenyan village at age 98, holds court on a low stool outside her thatched cooking hut. There is a spirit that emanates from the weathered woman, who has arms like tree bark and cloudy white eyes. Until recently, she was the primary caretaker for her great-grandson, a 12-year-old orphan named Motia.

One by one, Nduku's family members passed on. Her daughter was the first to go, followed by her four sons, all felled by AIDS. Then her granddaughter, Motia's mother, passed on, so that the aged woman was the only one left to look after the boy.

"I was taking care of this orphan—doing the washing, changing diapers, cooking for him, doing anything possible until I lost my sight," Nduku says in her native Kamba language. She used to till the fields on her family's land in Tala, and she probably would still be doing so were it not for her blindness, neighbors say.

Nduku is part of Africa's vast network of aging women, grandmothers who have helped keep families together as the middle generation is being lost to AIDS. Among the 12 million orphans now in sub-Saharan Africa, it is estimated that 40 to 60 percent live in households headed by grannies.

Nduku's village is just an hour's drive from Nairobi, yet it stands worlds apart in the slow drone of its rural life. Oxen still pull the plows in Tala, where most residents survive on the maize, beans and vegetables they are able to grow themselves.

On the day of our visit, Nduku is ensconced outside her hut in the scalding mid-day sun. She wears a blue and yellow flowered dress and a blue cap that falls behind her ears, exposing a broad expanse of forehead. As we arrive, an audience of some 40 curious neighbors quickly materializes

SARA NDUKU

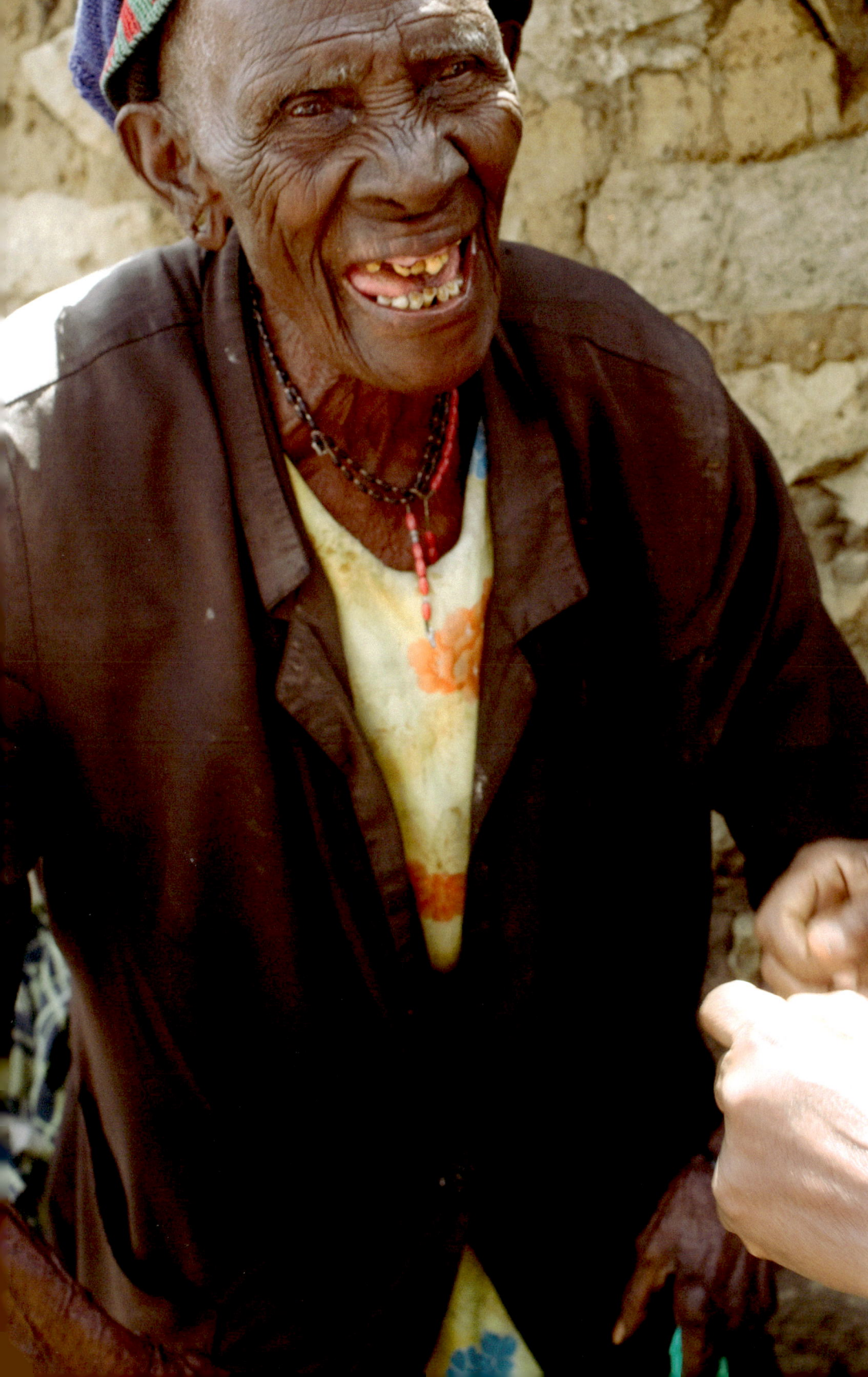

GO GO GRANNIES: AFRICA'S WELL OF HOPE 91

from the bush, for white-faced visitors are rare in this little town.

The aged lady rises to the occasion, gingerly lifting herself from her stool and bending forward, elbows in the air. She begins to sway her slender hips in a traditional Kamba dance and to chant a song of joy and appreciation. A high-pitched tone issues from the traditional Kamba whistle that is lodged in the side of her mouth, balancing there like a cigar. The neighborhood women join in, dancing and ululating in unison. The old lady is enthralled.

"In all my life, I have never had such an audience with a white person," she says. "It's a miracle."

Stephen Lewis, the former U.N. Envoy for AIDS in Africa, is a champion of these care-giving grannies, whom he calls "the heroes of Africa."

"They bury their own children and then care for their grandchildren," Lewis says. "In a magnificent demonstration of resilience, they hold communities together."

Nduku says she was happy to be able look after her great grandson. But for many of these women, being pressed into service as caretakers in their later years is a hardship,

SARA NDUKU, "THE DANCING GRANNY," GREETS HER VISITORS.

as well as a joy. Often they are widows with little or no means of support.

"I mothered my own children, and they died and left me with this burden. I have no strength now," says 65-year-old Hannah Wanyari, who has four grandchildren in her charge in Gilgil, a farming community some 100 miles northwest of Tala.

Wanyari is a member of Gilgil's "Granny Club," one of many community groups that have sprung to life to teach these resilient women new life skills and provide them with social support. This group, facilitated by social worker Teresa Wahito, has had some success in helping these women gain greater economic independence. As a result of its efforts, more than 50 orphans who might otherwise be abandoned or grow up in shelters are now living at home with their grandmothers, Wahito says.

ABOVE: TERESA WAHITO (LEFT), COORDINATOR FOR THE "GRANNY CLUB," WITH MARY MUTHUNI DURING A CLUB MEETING

RIGHT: GRANNY CLUB MEMBERS (LEFT TO RIGHT) HANNAH WANJIKU, MONICA MUMBI, AND HANNAH WANYARI

On a scorching summer afternoon, we leave downtown Gilgil to join a gathering of Granny Club members at a home in the parched plains several miles to the north. Wanyari and three other grannies, all wizened women in their 50s and 60s, climb with difficulty into the bed of our Land Rover for a ride out to the isolated mud hut of 57-year-old Anne Mbithe. The women chatter like magpies in the rumbling truck, gaily exchanging the day's news, as we head north into the steep hills, then drive off the road through massive gulleys and rocky fields swept clean by cattle and sheep over-grazing. Mbithe, tall and buxom, greets us with a hug and a buss on each cheek. She is wearing a white kerchief and white wrap—signs of her widowhood. Her hut is papered with pictures of Jesus and has an overpowering smell of sheep. The animals can be heard bleating in the bedroom next door.

Most of the women gathered here make a living tilling crops—maize, tomatoes, greens and other vegetables—on shambas, or family farms, owned by others. For a day's labor in the fields, they may earn the equivalent of about $1.50, enough to buy some maize meal and cooking fat to feed their families for a day

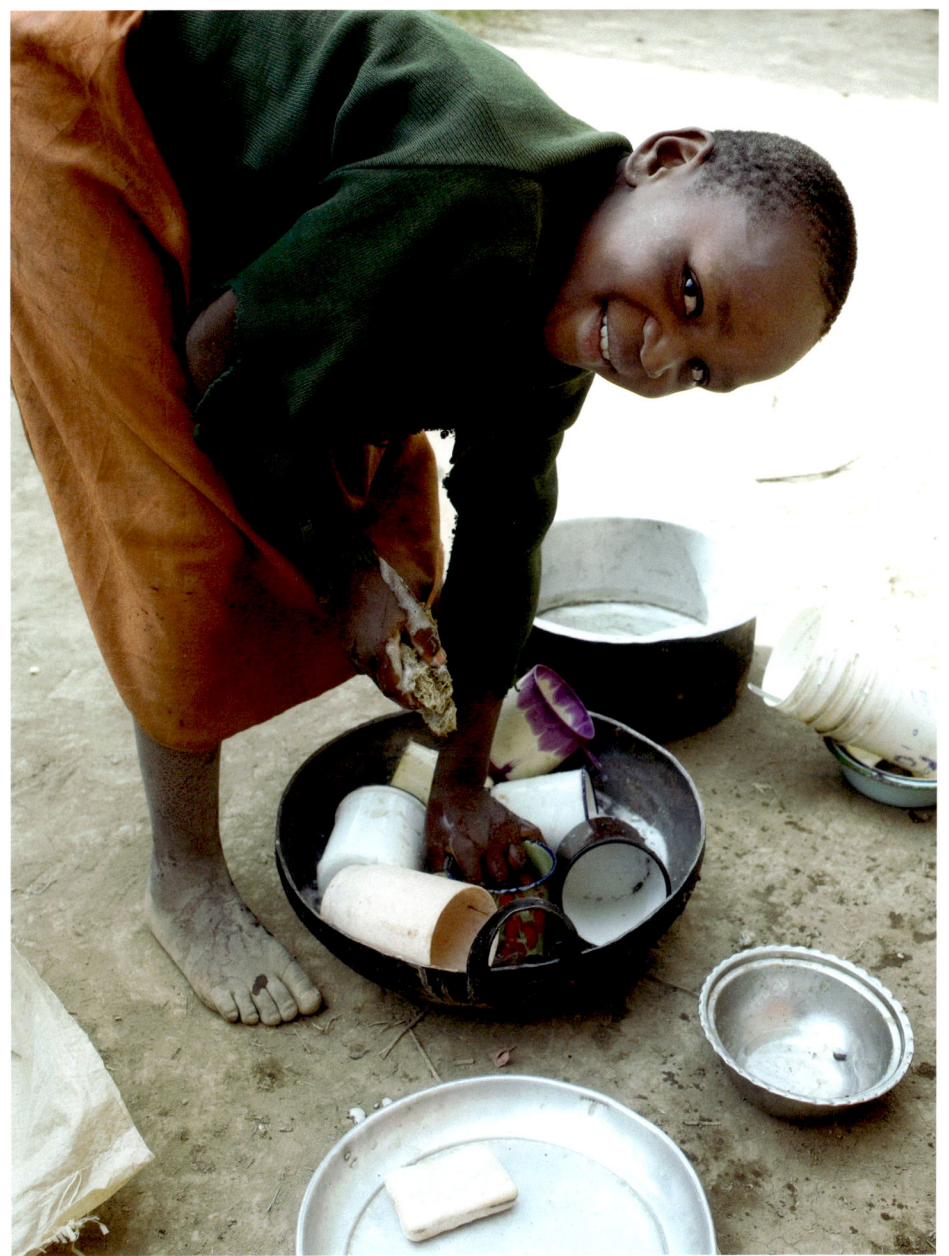

LEFT: PRISCILLA LIVES IN KIBERA, WHERE SHE CARES FOR EIGHT GRANDCHILDREN.

RIGHT: WANJIKO, GRANDDAUGHTER OF ANNE MBITHE, WASHES DISHES.

or two. Wanyari says field work is hard, especially at her age, but she has no other options.

"There are children in the house to feed, and there is nothing else I can do," she says in her native Kikuyu language. But now the land is dry, for the rains have yet to come, and there is not even work to be had. So on days like this, there is little to eat. Still, hospitality comes before poverty, as is often the case in Kenya, and these generous grannies don't allow us to leave without sharing a meal of rice and beans with them.

Most of the women in the group have suffered as a result of Kenya's ethnic strife. All, except Mbithe, are members of the dominant Kikuyu tribe whose economic and political power have fueled resentment among Kenya's smaller tribes. Following Kenya's disputed presidential election in late 2007, this tribal enmity surfaced with astonishing force, as violent clashes left more than 1,000 people dead and forced hundreds of thousands from their homes.

Many of the women in the group already had been displaced by previous tribal conflicts. For instance, Monica Mumbi, a frail 65-year-old who is missing her front teeth, says that in 2000 she was forced from her home in Nakuru, about 10 miles to the north, and had to restart her life in Gilgil with nothing. She lost her daughter to tuberculosis, the most common infection associated with HIV, and now has the daughter's three children to care for.

The Gilgil women supplement their incomes by weaving baskets, purses and hats, spending two or three days to fashion a basket that might fetch $3 in the market. As we sit in a circle and chat, their hands are deftly at work, pulling threads of colored wool through strands of sisal rope. The final results are works of arts, beautiful but sturdy.

To help support the children, the Granny Club is branching out into other income-producing businesses. The group has acquired

ABOVE: THREE MEMBERS OF A LARGE GRANNY GROUP IN THIKA

GO GO GRANNIES: AFRICA'S WELL OF HOPE 97

some land to grow vegetables for sale in the market, with the hope that as the business thrives, so will the youngsters.

Outside the hut, Mbithe's grandson, 13-year-old Benjamin, tells us he has had nothing to eat today except for a cup of tea in the morning before school. He is neatly dressed in a striped shirt and blue pants and speaks passable English, unlike his granny and her friends, who never attended school, where English is routinely taught.

Benjamin fetches the water for the family, trekking 10 kilometers every day into the hills to buy a jerry can for the eqivalent of two cents. His 9-year-old sister, Wanjiko, is barefoot, lathered in dirt, as she cheerfully washes out pots and does her chores around the house. Benjamin says he hopes one day to become a teacher. With his granny's support, he is able to keep that dream alive.

BENJAMIN, GRANDSON OF ANNE MBITHE

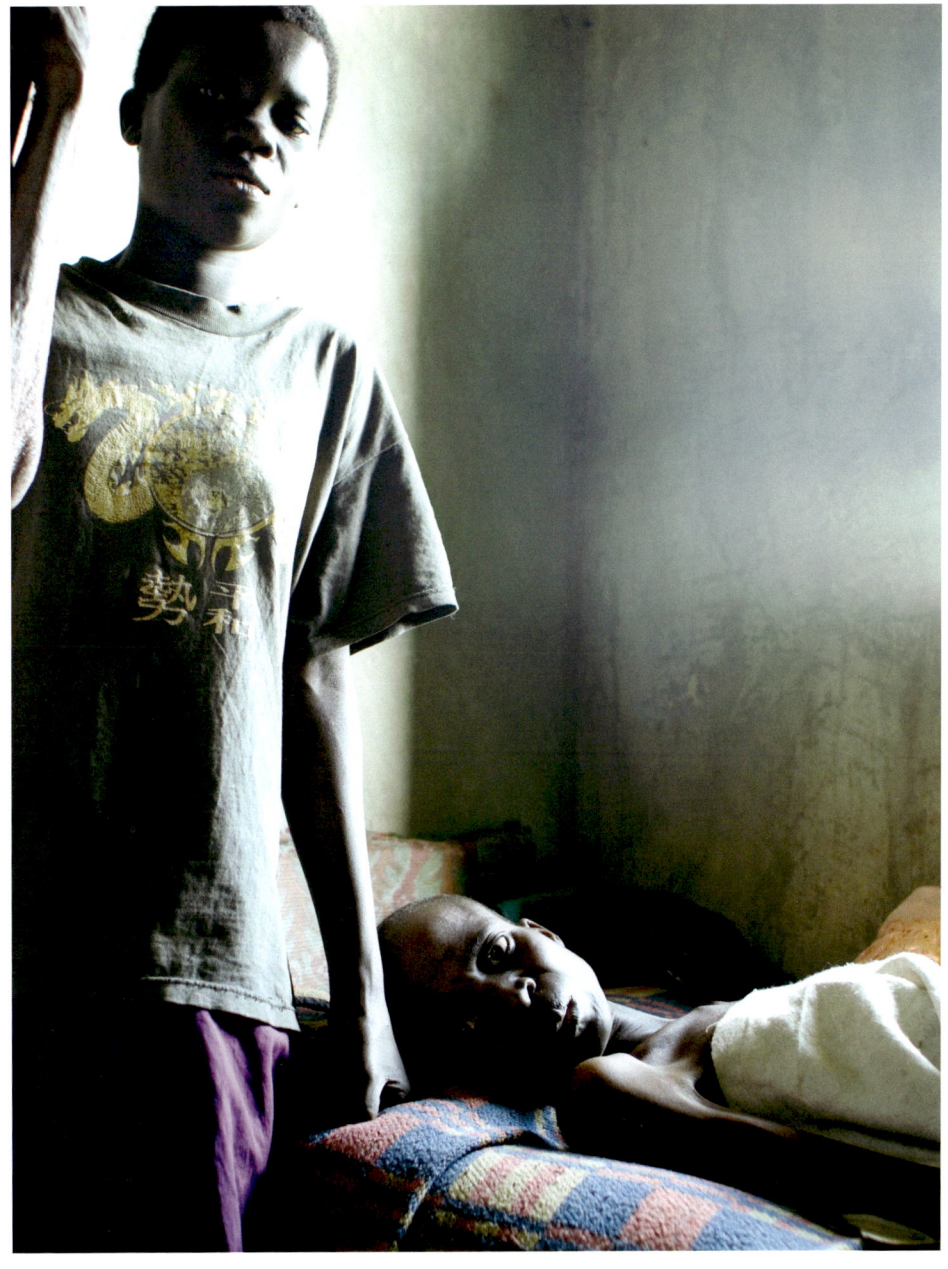

FACING PAGE: AT AGE 91, PAULLINA BECAME THE SOLE CARETAKER FOR 16 GRANDCHILDREN. THE LAST OF HER 12 CHILDREN, JANE (ABOVE RIGHT), DIED SIX WEEKS AFTER THIS PHOTO WAS TAKEN. JANE LEFT BEHIND FOUR ORPHANS, INCLUDING A TEENAGE DAUGHTER (ABOVE LEFT).

100 GO GO GRANNIES: AFRICA'S WELL OF HOPE

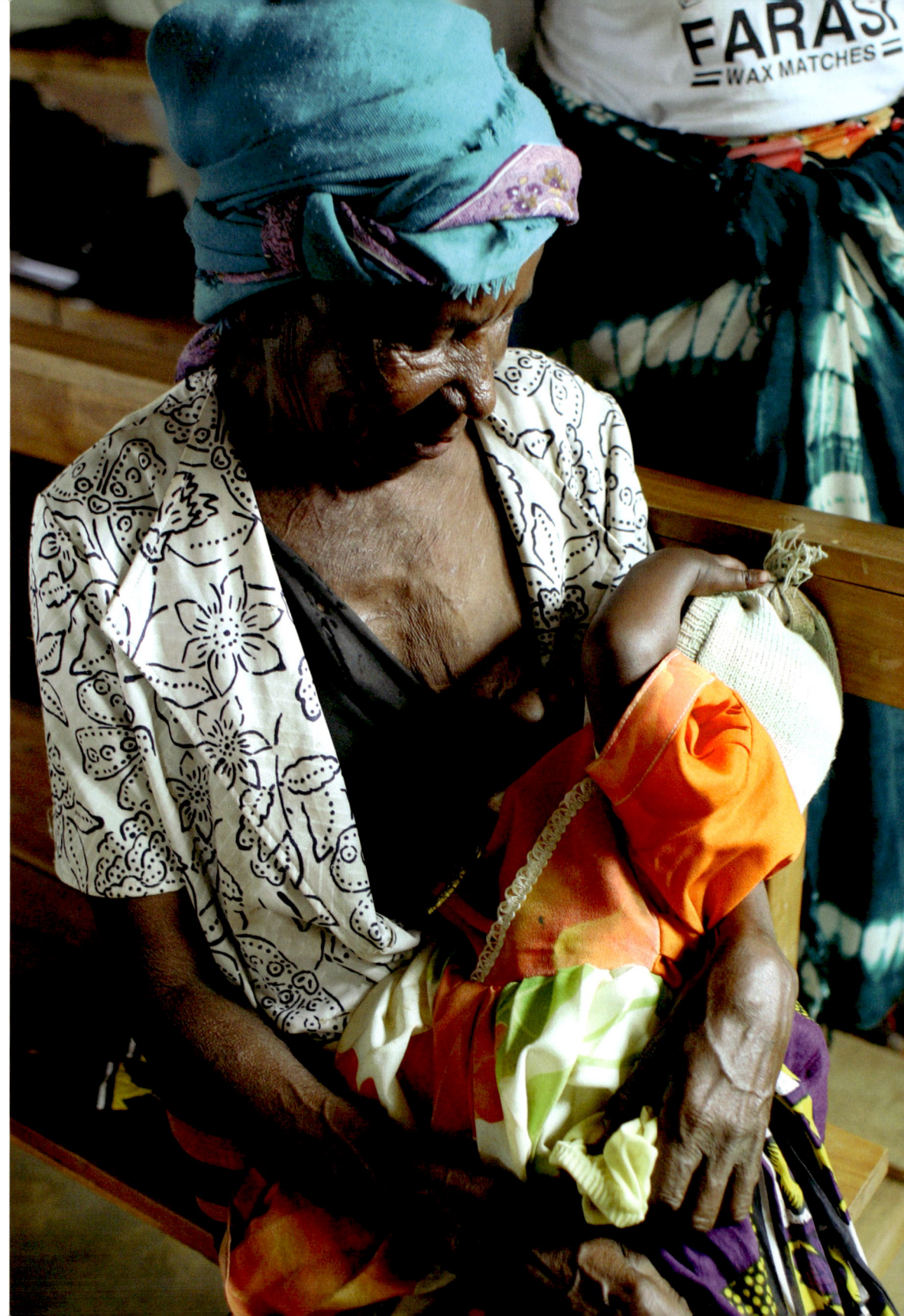

RIGHT: A GRANNY IN HER 60s, LIVING IN THE PARCHED HILLS NEAR KITUI, WAS ABLE TO NURSE HER GRANDCHILD AFTER HER DAUGHTER DIED OF AIDS. SHE HAD NO OTHER OPTION, SHE SAYS, AS SHE WAS TOO POOR TO BUY A COW TO SUPPLY MILK.

FACING PAGE: A WOMAN IN MACHAKOS BREAKS ROCKS USED IN CONSTRUCTION FOR THE EQUIVALENT OF 75 CENTS PER WHEELBARROW-LOAD, EARNING ENOUGH TO SEND HER 10-YEAR-OLD, ORPHANED GRANDDAUGHTER TO SCHOOL.

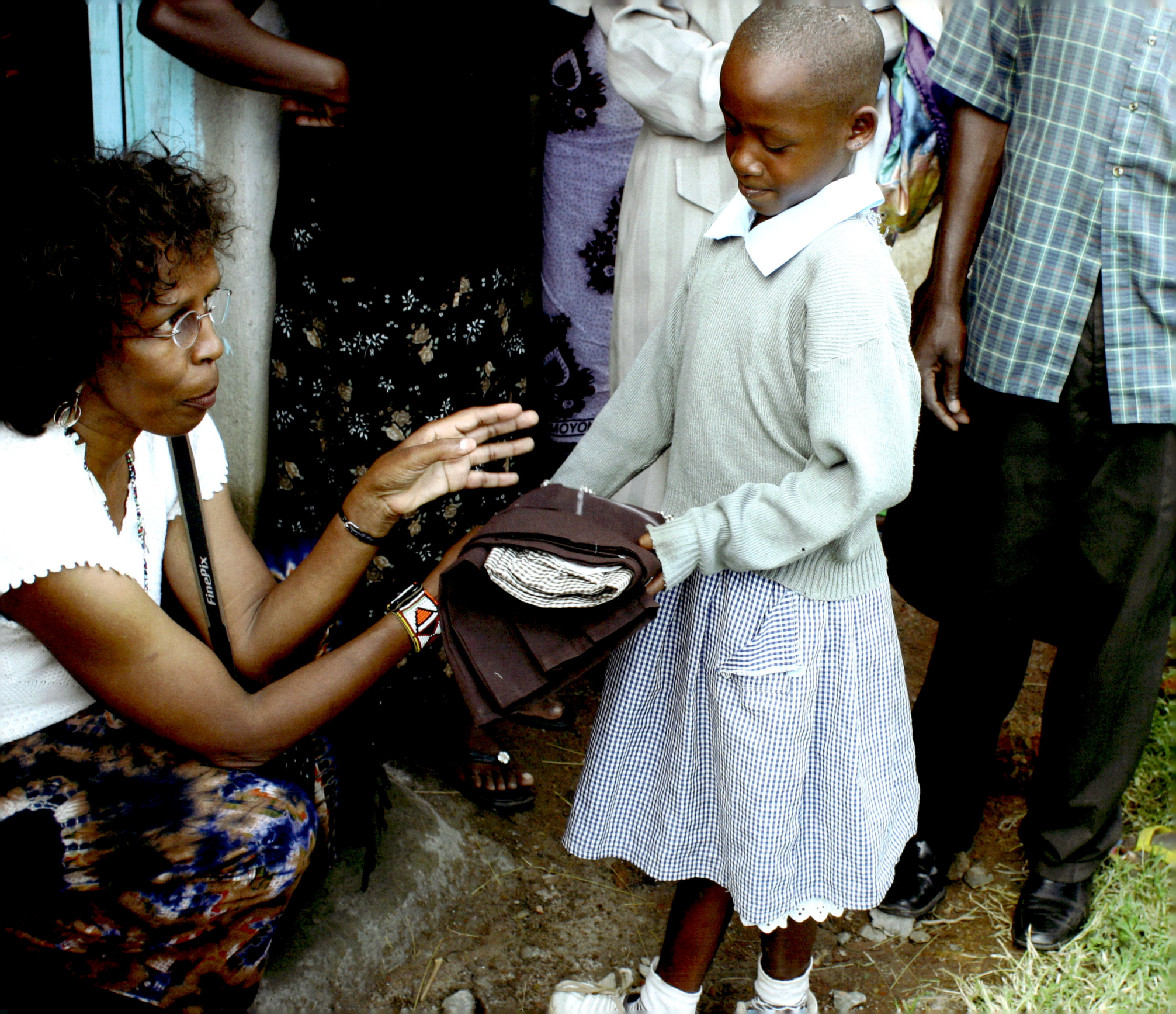

mama natasha and her brood

She came to see herself as the "death child," the one who brought the family down. "My aunt and uncle said I killed my parents. They said if I came closer to them and their children, I would cause death to them."

That was how Lillian Adhiambo had to cope with the loss of her parents to AIDS when she was just 12 years old. She was living in Butula, a poor, rural village in western Kenya near the Ugandan border. She was an only child, cast to the winds by the stigma of AIDS.

She went to live with her grandmother who was hard put to support her. "I once wore a torn shirt to school, and they ridiculed me," Adhiambo recalls. "They don't understand the experience the child is passing through and why they have that torn shirt. Teachers treated me with arrogance because I was an orphan."

One day in church, Adhiambo heard tell of a program supported by "Mama Natasha," also known as Natasha Martin.

Martin, an immunologist and AIDS researcher, happened to be visiting Butula one day in the late 1990s to make a presentation about her work in developing new therapies for HIV/AIDS. She was part of a research team then at the University of California, San Francisco, now widely known for its AIDS prevention, treatment and research programs. While in Butula, Martin noticed a group of children aimlessly milling about. It was a school day, and she wondered out loud why these youngsters weren't in class. She discovered they were orphans who couldn't afford the primary school fees, which then amounted to about $50 per child, including uniforms and books.

"MAMA NATASHA" PASSES OUT SCHOOL UNIFORMS
IN A PROJECT SPONSORED BY GRACE USA.

MAMA NATASHA AND HER BROOD

"It was unthinkable to me that these kids couldn't go to school," says Martin, a Barbados native who comes from a family of educators. "I made the rash statement that I'd make sure they went to school."

And so, in that one impulsive moment, she became the adopted mother of some 200 orphans who are now in various stages of their education. Martin went on to create a nonprofit organization, GRACE USA (the Grassroots Alliance for Community Education), to support grassroots projects in Kenya fighting HIV/AIDS. In December 2008, the organization received a three-year, $2.8 million grant from the U.S. President's Emergency Plan for AIDS Relief (PEPFAR) to provide care and support for orphans and vulnerable children. GRACE works with a broad-array of community-based projects in Africa, including programs to educate Maasai midwives on HIV prevention, to train people with HIV/AIDS to raise dairy goats and to empower unemployed youth by teaching them marketable computer skills. Martin continues to support her adoptees, raising $250,000 in 2008 alone to help assure that they remain in school.

NATASHA MARTIN (RIGHT) MEETS WITH A GROUP OF MAASAI MIDWIVES (FACING PAGE) AND OTHERS IN THE COMMUNITY.

"These are the future leaders of Kenya, and we have to help get them there," she says.

Adhiambo, now 21, is among the first group of Martin's adoptees to attend college. She is the only girl from her village of about 15,000 to go to a university and the first member of her family with any education beyond elementary school, she says proudly.

"This is an opportunity that nobody is believing—even my uncles. They are not believing their eyes," she says.

Adhiambo tells us her story over coffee at an American-style mall in Nairobi, where she is studying education at Kenyatta University. She's smartly dressed with a black shawl thrown over a belted print top and skirt. She has a broad face, framed by carefully shaped corn rows. She lives by herself in a small, rented house in Nairobi, visiting "Mama Natasha" whenever her adopted mother is in town.

ABOVE: LILLIAN ADHIAMBO

LEFT: A CHILD AT A GRACE-SPONSORED SUPPORT GROUP MEETING NEAR KITUI

She says she came to think of herself as a "death child" after reading a poem of that name by one of Martin's other adoptees, Charles Ouma:

The Death Child

Death followed me everywhere.
First it was my father.
Then my mother.
I went to stay with my uncle.
He too died. I moved to grandmother
And she sure died.
I was afraid.
It was said I was a bad omen.
I carried death.
I was called a death child.
I almost believed.
But I often asked myself.
Why hasn't Mama Natasha died?
Why is Mama Mary still alive?
Yet they love me so much?

Like Ouma, Adhiambo was able to move past the shadows of her family to make something of her life. Now, when the young woman goes back to her community of Butula, she is a bit of a celebrity there.

"My life could be nowhere, but now good things are coming," she says with a broad smile.

Martin Okello, whom she refers to as her "brother," also joins us at the mall. Mama Natasha's 200 adoptees see themselves as siblings, and they support one another as part of this large, surrogate family. Okello, 21, is wearing a San Francisco 49ers cap and a shirt from the Monterey Bay Aquarium in Monterey, Calif.—a far cry from the days when he was shoeless, dressed in rags.

"We were starving. I had no blanket or sheet to cover myself at night. We had nothing," he recalls of the days after his father's passing. "If you had seen me, you would have run away."

After Okello's father died of AIDS in 1998, his uncle took control of the father's property, though it was the boy's rightful inheritance under Kenyan law. Okello and his three sisters were left destitute.

"The first year they (the uncle and his family) cultivated the harvest and took it away and left us nothing," he says. He couldn't afford the school fees but was desperate to stay in class. So he would cut down trees, burn the wood down to charcoal and bicycle 30 kilometers to a nearby town where the cooking fuel would fetch a higher price. It took

MAMA NATASHA'S ADOPTEES MARTIN OKELLO (FAR RIGHT) AND LAZARUS NANZALA, WHO SAYS THAT "HAVING THE OPPORTUNITY OF AN EDUCATION IS A MIRACLE."

him three weeks to cobble together $4 so he could take his exams. He was just 12 years old.

"I looked at myself then as a person locked in a room, full of dirtiness. When Mama Natasha came, that door opened. I recognized what was wrong and what was right."

He mustered the courage to fight his uncle in court and regain his rightful claim to his father's land. Today, he attends the University of Nairobi, where he is studying journalism and mass communications.

He, Adhiambo and their adopted siblings say they hope to complete their education and then return to their village to help lift up other orphans, so they don't have to suffer, too.

RIGHT AND FACING PAGE: THROUGH A GRACE-SUPPORTED PROJECT, MAASAI MIDWIVES LEARN HOW TO PROTECT THEMSELVES AND THEIR CLIENTS FROM HIV.

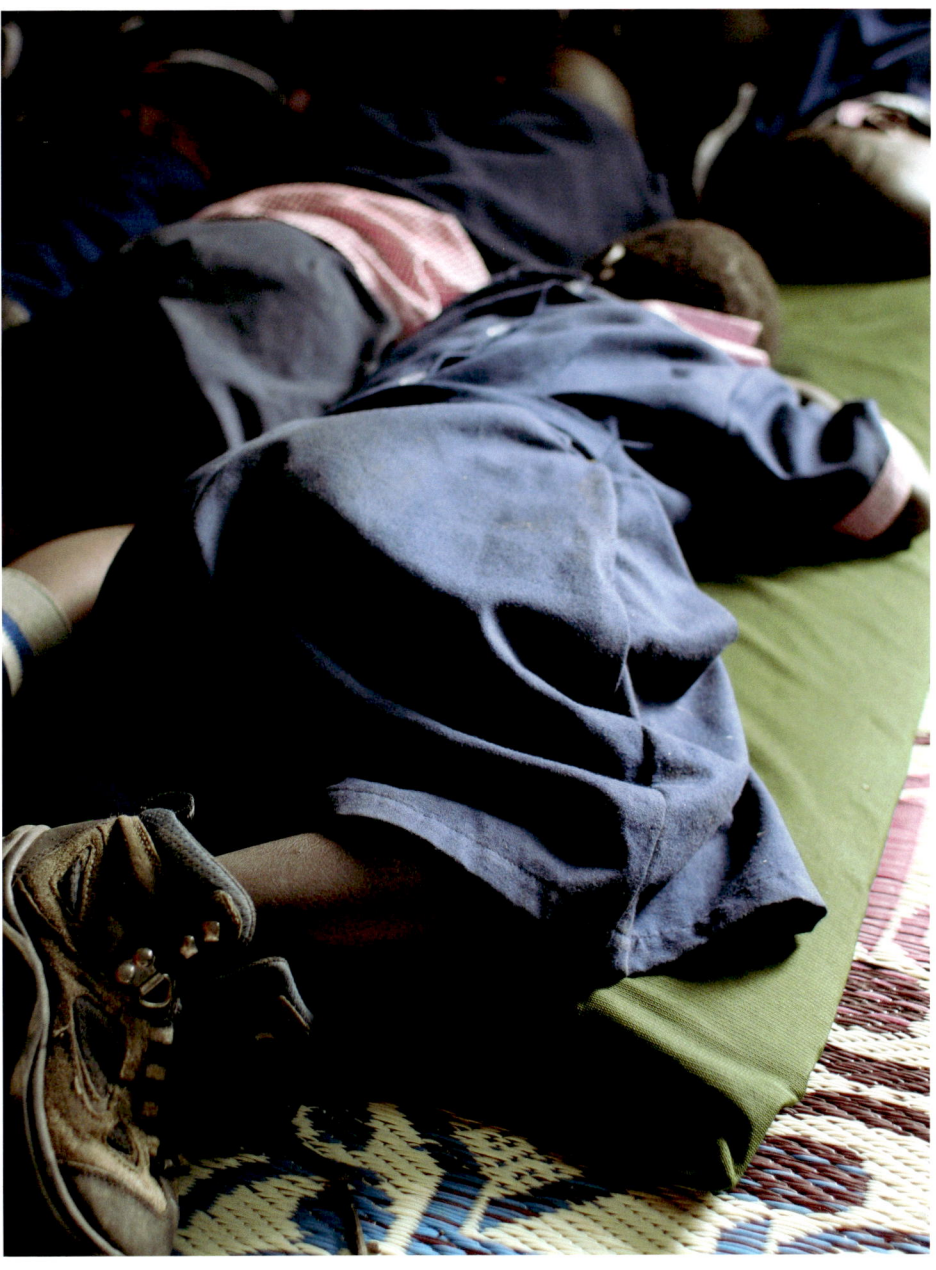

LEFT: WOMEN WITH THE SINGLE MOTHERS ASSOCIATION OF KENYA LEARN TAILORING TO SUPPORT THEMSELVES. WHILE THEY'RE IN CLASS, THEIR CHILDREN NAP (ABOVE).

114 MAMA NATASHA AND HER BROOD

RIGHT: WITH NATASHA MARTIN'S HELP, MARY STARTED A PHARMACY TO BENEFIT ORPHANS (FACING PAGE) IN HER VILLAGE IN WESTERN KENYA.

a brief chronology of the epidemic

1981 — In June 1981, AIDS is officially recognized as a new disease by the U.S. Centers for Disease Control and Prevention following reports in New York and Los Angeles of a number of gay men who are ill with a rare pneumonia. In sub-Saharan Africa, the epidemiologic data suggest the spread of the disease began in the late 1970s.

1983 — Dr. Luc Montagnier and colleagues at the Institut Pasteur in France report that they have isolated a new virus, which they suggest might be the cause of AIDS.

1984 — Dr. Robert Gallo of the National Cancer Institute reports in *Science* magazine in May that he has isolated the virus which causes AIDS.

1985 — The first International AIDS Conference is held in Atlanta. Participants still widely discredit reports of a growing epidemic in Africa.

1986 — Dr. Peter Piot leads a team of scientists to Zaire (now the Congo), where they report finding the first evidence that AIDS is transmitted in a heterosexual population.

1987 — In a landmark paper published in November in *Science* magazine, researchers report that the number of AIDS cases in central Africa is exploding. The study makes it clear that the transmission of the disease is heterosexual.

The U.S. Food and Drug Administration approves the first anti-AIDS drug, AZT.

1996 — At the International AIDS Conference in Vancouver, British Columbia, scientists report that a three-drug combination of newly developed antivirals, known as protease inhibitors, could knock down the virus. The drugs usher in a new era in which AIDS is transformed from a death sentence to a manageable disease. But the drugs' high cost—more than $10,000 a year—puts them out of reach for patients in the developing world.

The Joint United Nations Programme on HIV/AIDS (UNAIDS) is formed to combine the efforts of 10 U.N. organizations in fighting the global pandemic.

A BRIEF CHRONOLOGY OF THE EPIDEMIC   117

2000

2001 The U.N. Security Council holds its first summit on the disease in January. This year also marks the start of a global movement to provide universal access to anti-AIDS drugs. It is spurred by the development of generic copies of the medications, produced by the India-based company Cipla.

In June, the United Nations convenes a General Assembly special session in which world leaders declare their commitment to provide support to combat global AIDS.

2002 The Global Fund to Fight AIDS, Tuberculosis and Malaria, an independent group with partners in the public and private sectors, is launched to fight these three killers.

2003 President George W. Bush announces a new 5-year, $15 billion program, known as the President's Emergency Plan for AIDS Relief (PEPFAR), to finance treatment and prevention programs in 15 target countries, including 12 in Africa.

The World Health Organization launches its "3-by-5 Initiative," which aims to provide treatment to 3 million people by 2005. The effort falls short of its objective but helps triple the number of people with access to drugs—from 400,000 to 1.3 million.

2006 The Bill and Melinda Gates Foundation awards $287 million—the largest investment to date—in an effort to develop an AIDS vaccine, a goal that has consistently eluded scientists.

2008 Some 3 million people in the developing world, most of them in Africa, now receive treatment with antiretroviral drugs. Still, at least double that number still need these vital anti-AIDS drugs and do not receive them.

2009 The epidemic continues to outpace prevention and treatment efforts. For every two people on antiretroviral drugs, there are five people who are newly infected with the virus. That translates into 6,000 to 7,000 new infections every day.

The fight to contain AIDS is just beginning.

acknowledgments

We are grateful to the many individuals and families in Kenya who opened their doors and their hearts to us. Though they have suffered much hardship, they showed enormous courage, determination and generosity of spirit. We are grateful, too, to those who have devoted their lives to lifting up others and who were of great assistance in making this book come to life: Monica Ngumi and Eliud Muema, Jill and Angus Simpson, John Adoli, Father Daniel Kiriti, Jecinta Gakahu, Jane Kinuthia, Teresa Wahito, Heidi Pidcoke, Eric Oberholtzer, Natasha Martin and Patricia Sewe. Thanks to Catherine Wanjohi and the women of LifeBloom Services International for allowing us into the intimate circle of their support group. Thanks also to the folks at the Village Enterprise Fund for giving us an inside look at their programs and the families they support in Nairobi.

Thanks to the creative energies of our editor, Jonathan Rabinovitz, and our designers, Doug da Silva and Annemarie Clark of Clark Creative Group. Thanks also to Karen's mentor, Frank Espada, who first suggested creating this book.

We feel very fortunate to have had the support of so many family members and friends. We are particularly grateful to Lenore Richter for her generosity and love and for always being there to help.

Many thanks to Jay and Shaina Hammer for tolerating Ruthann's long absences while in Africa and for their love and support throughout. To Jeff Johnson, for his love, patience and support for this project and for his willingness to carry Karen's camera gear just about anywhere. To Pastor Schuyler Rhodes and the community members of Temple United Methodist Church in San Francisco for their willingness to help children they will never meet.

To Karen's parents, James and Dorothy Hadley, who contributed to this project on faith and are seeing the results from heaven.

Thanks finally to the children of the Saidia and Mji Wa Neema orphanages, who must live the reality of the AIDS epidemic every day, yet continue to kindle hope in all of us.

about the author and photographer

Ruthann Richter has been writing about medical issues, including HIV/AIDS, since the early 1980's. She holds a master's degree in journalism from Stanford University and has received awards for her reporting from the American Cancer Society, the Association of American Medical Colleges, the Council for Advancement and Support of Education and the National Alliance for the Mentally Ill. She first traveled to Africa in 2004, when she became gripped by the human devastation of AIDS and felt compelled to help through her writings, presentations and fundraising. In addition to her Africa projects, she is the director of media relations at Stanford University School of Medicine, where she works with media from around the world and covers HIV/AIDS issues. She lives in Palo Alto, Calif., with her husband, Jay, and daughter, Shaina.

Karen Ande has been chronicling the AIDS epidemic in sub-Saharan Africa since 2002. She has traveled extensively as a volunteer with NGO's in Kenya and Rwanda, photographing community-based projects and the people they serve. Whether working in rural villages or city slums, she has been moved and inspired by the people who daily face the challenges of AIDS and its impact on those they know and love. Not content to observe, she and her collaborator, Ruthann Richter, have raised funds to help support the people and projects introduced in these pages. Her photographs have been featured widely in newspapers, magazines, the Web, television and in solo exhibits. Karen lives with her husband, Jeff Johnson, and two cats, Morani and Magnificat, in San Francisco.

resources

SUPPORT FOR ORGANIZATIONS FEATURED IN THE BOOK

Firelight Foundation • www.firelightfoundation.org
Supports grassroots organizations working with families and communities to help children orphaned and made vulnerable by HIV/AIDS and poverty.

GRACE USA (Grassroots Alliance for Community Education) • www.graceusa.org
Mentors a vibrant network of community-based organizations dealing with AIDS in Africa.

International Partners in Mission • www.ipm-connections.org
Supports the work of Kibera Hamlets, among other groups.

Kenya Help • www.kenyahelp.us
Supports the work of Father Kiriti and the Catholic Church in Naivasha, including the Mji Wa Neema orphanage, HIV/AIDS outreach program and a new girls high school.

Orphan Support League • www.orphansupportleague.org
Provides funds for the Saidia Children's Home in Gilgil.

Village Enterprise Fund • www.villageef.org
Provides training, seed capital and mentoring for small income-generating businesses in sub-Saharan Africa.

OTHER ORGANIZATIONS

A Global Connection • www.aglobalconnection.org
Supports clinics serving HIV-positive children and families in Rwanda.

Asante Africa Foundation • www.asanteafrica.org
Helps provide quality education to East African children by partnering with local activists committed to change.

FACE AIDS • www.faceaids.org
Mobilizes college students to fight AIDS in Africa and operates an income-generating project together with AIDS associations in Rwanda.

Stephen Lewis Foundation • www.stephenlewisfoundation.org
Supports community organizations that provide care to sick women, help orphans and other children affected by AIDS and sustain grandmothers caring for orphans.

Partners in Health • www.pih.org
Provides quality health care for the poorest of the poor in Africa and elsewhere, using a community-based approach.